Praise for *The Ultimate LinkedIn® Messaging Guide*

No one spends more time on studying how to use LinkedIn to engage prospects. Of all the social sites, LinkedIn is the most useful, but only if you know how to use it. If you want to use LinkedIn, read and apply Daniel Disney's book.

Anthony Iannarino – Author of *The Only Sales Guide You'll Ever Need, The Lost Art of Closing* **and** *Eat Their Lunch*

Daniel is an authority in the Social Selling space and this book further solidifies that notion. You will get actionable advice and more insight than you ever dreamed possible when it comes to LinkedIn and the social game you need to be playing. Brilliant read! Pick up this book and start changing the game.

Dale Dupree – Leader of *The Sales Rebellion*

LinkedIn holds the golden keys to sales at all levels. Daniel Disney knows how to use the keys to open doors and close business. There are hundreds of LinkedIn "experts," but Daniel doesn't just talk the talk, he walks the walk. From creating The Daily Sales to closing The Million Pound Sale, Daniel's easy to follow tips will give you new ways to improve your LinkedIn results.

Alison Edgar – Author of *Secrets of Successful Sales*

LinkedIn is vital for your business, yet most people are not using it effectively. The UK's Number 1 Social Selling expert, Daniel Disney, solves this problem by showing you easy-to-implement techniques and tips that will make your LinkedIn profile shine and help you generate more awareness and revenue for your business. I've read many LinkedIn books, and this is my favourite. Don't delay and buy your copy now to make a difference in your business.

Niraj Kapur - Expert Sales Coach, Trainer and Author – Amazon bestseller *Everybody Works in Sales*

This book unlocks simple but powerful strategies for winning on LinkedIn. Whether you are a seasoned LinkedIn pro or a green LinkedIn newbie, this book is for you. My favourites were the 25 message templates which are jam-packed with instructions for when and how to use them.

Daniel Disney is the real deal; he has real followers, real successes, and is the number one influencer on LinkedIn. That stands him out from the LinkedIn crowd as the go-to expert. If you're going to listen to one person on the subject of LinkedIn, make it Daniel.

Better still, buy his book, read it on the plane/train/automobile (he has packed it with content, not waffle), and start applying it the moment you land.

Gavin Ingham - Founder of #IAM10 & Author of *Be More, Do More, Sell More*

Daniel teaches me something every time I read his content on LinkedIn, and what I learned after his LinkedIn/Social Selling Masterclass has helped me generate some great results on social media. After reading his new book, *The Ultimate LinkedIn Messaging Guide*, I had no doubt straight away that this would be the reference guide for so many sellers out there.

You have given the roadmap for all to follow, the question you will pose to every reader is, what will they do with these golden nuggets? Will they make their own million-pound sale or watch while others make theirs?!

Steve Knapp – Founder of *The Sales Growth Club*, Expert Sales Coach, Trainer & Consultant

Although I had the good fortune to have worked directly for LinkedIn, few people on or at LinkedIn impressed me with the frequency, consistency and relevancy of content to inspire salespeople to leverage social media as much as Daniel Disney.

His dedication to providing valuable content to the world's sales community is second to none. What I love about this book is that it gets deep, tactical and practical with excellent tips you can leverage to inspire greater confidence in your sales efforts on LinkedIn. Highly recommend reading and sending around your team.

James Ski, Former LinkedIn Director and now Founder & CEO of *Sales Confidence* – the world's largest B2B Sales community

In a sea of wishy-washy blog posts and crappy video content from so-called "social guru's," Daniel has bucked the trend and put together a step-by-step guide to engineering success on LinkedIn that anyone can follow.

Will Barron – Host of *The Salesman Podcast*

It's rare that a book can connect with you as a friend, mentor you as a teacher, correct you as a parent and encourage you as a colleague. This book does exactly that. Daniel's informal voice and delivery make this book an easy read that you simply cannot put down. Even as I read it, I knew I'd be referencing the content, templates and how-to tactics over and over again; it will be front-and-centre on my bookshelf.

Of particular note are the many templates that Daniel provides, along with the use-case instructions and explanations for each of them. Whether you're a novice or an industry veteran, you WILL get immediate value from them, and you WILL be using them over and over again. This book is a must-read and a must-share.

Darryl Praill – CMO at *VanillaSoft* & Host of *The INSIDE,*
Inside Sales Podcast

THE ULTIMATE LINKEDIN® MESSAGING GUIDE

THE ULTIMATE LINKEDIN® MESSAGING GUIDE

HOW TO USE WRITTEN, AUDIO, VIDEO AND IN MAIL MESSAGES TO START MORE CONVERSATIONS AND INCREASE SALES

DANIEL DISNEY

WILEY

Registered Offices
John Wiley & Sons, Inc., 111 River Street, Hoboken, NJ 07030, USA

John Wiley & Sons Ltd, The Atrium, Southern Gate, Chichester, West Sussex, PO19 8SQ, UK

Editorial Office
The Atrium, Southern Gate, Chichester, West Sussex, PO19 8SQ, UK

For details of our global editorial offices, customer services, and more information about Wiley products visit us at www.wiley.com.

Wiley also publishes its books in a variety of electronic formats and by print-on-demand. Some content that appears in standard print versions of this book may not be available in other formats.

Library of Congress Cataloging-in-Publication Data is Available:

ISBN 9781394185221 (Hardback)
ISBN 9781394187867 (ePDF)
ISBN 9781394187850 (ePub)

Cover Design and Image: Wiley

SKY10042008_020123

THIS BOOK IS DEDICATED TO FOUR PEOPLE:

Uncle Al – The man who inspired me to get into sales and taught me to be the best salesperson I could possibly be. Not a day goes by that I don't wish you were still here to guide me, to see what I've achieved and to read my book. I hope it would have made you proud.

Laurie – You stand by me whilst I put everything into my career. When I worked late nights and weekends trying to grow *The Daily Sales* and my *Social Selling Masterclass*, you did everything you could to make it as easy as possible for me. I'm so lucky to have you in my life, and I will do everything *I* can to provide the best possible life for you and our boys.

Joshua and Lewis – My two sons, you are the reason I work so hard and you are the ones who make it all worthwhile. I love you more than anything in this world and am so proud of you both and the wonderful men that you are becoming.

Thank you for being such a huge part of my world and being the driving force behind all I do.

CONTENTS

Dedication   *ix*

Foreword by Chris Murray   *xv*

About the Author   *xix*

Introduction   *xxiii*

Part 1   Prospecting With Messages   **1**

Chapter 1   Motivation To Message   3

Chapter 2   The Prospecting Maze   7

Chapter 3   Outbound Social Selling   13

Part 2   Research & Personalisation   **19**

Chapter 4   Why Aren't People Replying?   21

Chapter 5   Research, Personalisation & Relevance 25

Chapter 6   The One Thing To Avoid   31

Chapter 7   No One Likes Spam Messages   37

Part 3   LinkedIn Messaging Thoughts   **49**

Chapter 8   InMail VERSUS Message   51

Chapter 9   WHEN To Send A Message On LinkedIn   55

Chapter 10   One Size Doesn't Fit All   59

Part 4   Written LinkedIn Messages   **63**

Chapter 11   The Seven-Figure LinkedIn Message   65

Chapter 12   25 Written Sales Message Templates   81

Chapter 13   Top Written Message Tips   117

Part 5   Audio LinkedIn Messages   **119**

Chapter 14   Audio Voice Notes On LinkedIn   121

Chapter 15   How To Send Audio Voice Notes On LinkedIn   125

Chapter 16   The Two MOST IMPORTANT Components   129

Chapter 17   LinkedIn Audio Voice Notes Sales Scripts   133

Chapter 17a   BONUS CHAPTER – Audio Voice Notes 101   141

Part 6   Video LinkedIn Messages   **147**

Chapter 18   Video Messages On LinkedIn   149

Chapter 19   From Video To Sale In 24 Hours   153

Chapter 20   Ten Video Sales Message Scripts   159

Chapter 20a   BONUS CHAPTER – Sending LinkedIn
               Video Messages   169

Part 7   InMail Messages On Sales Navigator   **177**

Chapter 21   InMail Messages On LinkedIn   179

Chapter 22   InMail Subject Lines   183

Chapter 23   Ten InMail Sales Templates   185

Part 8   Follow Up, Replies & Converting To Sales   197

Chapter 24   What If They Don't Reply?   199

Chapter 25   Pick Up The Phone   203

Chapter 26   Conversation To Opportunity   207

Part 9   Bonus Chapters   211

Chapter 27   Pipeline Will Always Be King   213

Chapter 28   Ten Big LinkedIn & Sales Navigator Tips   219

Chapter 29   Social Selling Top Tips   227

Chapter 30   Building A Strong LinkedIn Profile   231

Chapter 31   Cold Calling Is Like Blockbuster   237

Chapter 32   Social Selling In 15 Minutes Per Day   241

Chapter 33   The ABC's Of Social Selling   245

Working with Daniel Disney   *251*

Acknowledgements   *259*

Recommended Reading   *265*

Index   *267*

FOREWORD BY CHRIS MURRAY

Author of *The Extremely Successful Salesman's Club*
and *Selling with EASE*

There are a couple of things I need to share with you about Daniel Disney before we start.

First of all – with regards to 'Social Selling' – he really knows what he's talking about. Secondly – with regards to life in general – he is one of the good guys.

And it's because of those two points, that – in this world of snake-oil salespeople and faux business gurus who are happy to take punters' hard-earned cash in exchange for advice that sounds great but is almost certainly destined to fail – Daniel Disney stands out from the crowd and is definitely worth taking notice of.

The first time I met Daniel was at a large, national sales event. We were both due to deliver our keynote speeches on the same day, and I was in the organiser's office, checking over a couple of things, when this polite young man peered round the door and introduced himself.

Back then, *The Daily Sales* hadn't been around too long – but even so, he'd already managed to attract a following that numbered in the hundreds of thousands.

Now, I'd seen people pay huge amounts of money to cultivate lists like that before – so I asked him:

"That's an impressive audience. How much of it did you buy?"

To which, with a genuine look of shock, Daniel responded:

"Buy an audience? I don't think I'd know how to!"

That statement, made with the honest naiveté of someone who wasn't aware of how many "thought leaders" cheat their way to popularity, told me everything I needed to know.

The man standing in front of me wasn't buying attention – completely the opposite – he was well on his way to mastering the art and science of Customer Attraction.

And when it comes to business development in the 21st century, customer attraction was the secret ingredient that only a successful few had worked out how to bake with.

What I didn't realise back then was that there was something else in the Daniel Disney recipe mix – he had started successfully combining Customer Attraction with effective Social Sales Interaction.

And shortly afterwards, that combination just exploded.

The thing is, because it all came so easily and naturally to him, Daniel didn't seem to realise how rare or magical those particular pieces of business knowledge were – or why so many people found them difficult to implement.

To most people, it was like watching him pull a sword out of a stone – which is a piece of cake if you're the one who can do it but the deepest of mysteries if you can't.

Thankfully, in this book – *The Ultimate LinkedIn Messaging Guide* – Daniel shares that knowledge with us.

This is an incredibly powerful and generous piece of writing; he takes us step-by-step through his system and then shares dozens of templates and examples so that everyone who reads this can hit the ground running as soon as they've finished it.

You can dip in and out of this book if you need to, but there's so much you'll miss out on if you do.

My best advice:

Devour this book – page by page – and then go through it again and make notes. Focus on your current sales objectives and prospects and use the information Daniel shares to design a complete sales strategy from start to finish. Then, when you have a new sales challenge or a fresh set of prospective customers, come back and check it out again.

Because every time you familiarise yourself with the wealth of information in his book – and the multiple applications of its content – you will be building a knowledge bank and sales toolbox that will give you a genuine advantage over a large majority of your competition.

To your success,

Chris Murray

ABOUT THE AUTHOR

Daniel Disney is on a mission to help everyone leverage LinkedIn to its full potential to grow their personal brands, grow their businesses, generate more leads and sell more.

What separates him from 99% of the LinkedIn experts and trainers out there is that his background is in sales, not marketing.

Whilst he has learned how to generate a very large amount of consistent, qualified inbound leads from LinkedIn, grow brands and reach millions of people through content, his passion and focus have always been, and will always be, selling.

Here are a few of his LinkedIn achievements:

- 100,000+ Personal LinkedIn Profile Followers
- 900,000+ LinkedIn Company Page Followers

- £25,000,000+ in Revenue from LinkedIn
- 400+ Articles Published on LinkedIn
- 150 Million+ Content Views Every Year
- 10,000+ New Followers Every Single Month
- No.1 Most Influential Sales Expert on LinkedIn 2018, 2019, 2020, 2021 & 2022

Not only has he achieved a lot on LinkedIn, but he continues to do this every single day, even as you're reading this book right now.

Daniel leverages LinkedIn and social selling to not only sell his hugely popular LinkedIn training programmes and international keynote talks, but he uses it to grow his business *The Daily Sales* and their sponsorship packages. Daniel utilises everything that you will read in this book to generate opportunities, grow relationships, close sales and manage accounts selling advertising space and media partnerships.

What you'll read in this book are tried, tested, proven and mastered techniques, strategies and tips for turning LinkedIn into a lead-generating and sales-closing machine.

For more information on Daniel and what he offers, along with daily social selling, LinkedIn, and sales tips, follow him on LinkedIn, Facebook, Twitter, and Instagram, subscribe to his YouTube channel, and check out his website:

www.danieldisney.online

THE ULTIMATE LINKEDIN SALES GUIDE

How to Use Digital and Social Selling to Turn LinkedIn into a Lead, Sales and Revenue Generating Machine.

BECOME A LINKEDIN POWER USER AND HARNESS THE POTENTIAL OF SOCIAL SELLING

With the impact of COVID, remote working has become big—and so has the use of digital/virtual sales tools. More sales teams want and need to understand how to use social media platforms like LinkedIn to sell, and most do not use them properly. *The Ultimate LinkedIn Sales Guide* is the go-to book and guide for utilising LinkedIn to sell. It covers all aspects of social and digital selling, including building the ultimate LinkedIn profile, using the searching functions to find customers, sending effective LinkedIn messages (written, audio & video), creating great content that generates sales, and all the latest tips and tricks, strategies and tools. With the right LinkedIn knowledge, you can attract customers and generate leads, improving your sales numbers from the comfort and safety of your computer.

No matter what you are selling, LinkedIn can connect you to buyers. If you're savvy, you can stay in touch with clients and generate more repeat sales, build trust, and create engaging content that will spread by word-of-mouth—the most powerful sales strategy around. This book will teach you how to do all that and more. In *The Ultimate LinkedIn Sales Guide*, you will learn how to:

- Use the proven Four Pillars of Social Selling Success to improve your existing LinkedIn activities or get started on a firm footing.
- Create the Ultimate LinkedIn Profile, complete with a strong personal brand that could catapult you to industry leader status.
- Generate leads using LinkedIn, then build and manage relationships with connected accounts to turn those leads into customers.
- Utilise little-known LinkedIn "power tools" to grow your network, send effective messages, and write successful LinkedIn articles,
- And so much more!

The Ultimate LinkedIn Sales Guide is a must-read for anyone wishing to utilise LinkedIn to improve sales.

INTRODUCTION

When I wrote my first book, *The Million-Pound LinkedIn Message*, I shared my story of how one single message helped me create and win a seven-figure sale worth over £1,000,000. At the time, the world of LinkedIn was a different place. There was only one way that you could send messages, and that was by written text. The following year, video messaging and audio voice note messaging launched and since then, the way people communicate on LinkedIn has changed dramatically.

Whilst written text-based messages are still incredibly effective (when done right), audio and video messages are now equally powerful.

There is also a fourth method of messaging that I didn't cover in the original book, and that's InMail, a premium message that you send to people you're not connected with through platforms like LinkedIn

Sales Navigator and LinkedIn Premium (which requires a monthly/yearly fee).

Like all forms of messaging, many salespeople, businesses, recruiters and LinkedIn users struggle to get replies and results from them. There are a number of reasons for this, which I'll cover in the book. But when you figure it out—when you start doing it right—it's then you begin to crack the LinkedIn code and see just how powerful it is.

Over the last ten years, I've used (and continue to use) all forms of messaging on LinkedIn, and to date, it has helped me close over £25,000,000 in sales. Not only that, but these messaging strategies and templates have helped companies and salespeople all over the world to create and close so many more.

In this revised edition, I'm going to include the original book, but I'm expanding it heavily to become the ultimate guide to LinkedIn messaging, helping you, your teams and your businesses master LinkedIn messaging to start more conversations, create more opportunities and, more importantly, drive more sales and revenue.

Not only does this book include real examples of successful messages, but it also includes over 50 message templates and scripts for written, audio, video and InMail messages. There are also QR codes throughout the book that will take you through to recorded examples of video and audio messages so you can see and hear them in full action.

I WANT TO END THIS INTRODUCTION WITH ONE QUICK FACT FOR YOU. . .

Some of your target prospects and ideal customers are waiting and willing to talk to you; they need what you are selling, and they have money to spend.

They won't, however, respond to a spammy message. They might not answer your call or read your email.

But send a good, well-crafted message on LinkedIn. . .

Well, that might just be what catches their eye and prompts them to talk to you.

PERSONALISED CONNECTION REQUESTS

To some extent, these count as messages, and if you send a personalised connection request with a note, that note becomes the first message in your conversation history with the prospect.

So, when they go into their messages, your personalised connection request will appear as a message (if they accept your connection request, that is).

NOW, THERE ARE A FEW THINGS TO CONSIDER. . .

Firstly, you SHOULD NOT personalise every request that you send (which is why I'm including this as a small segment at the beginning of this book).

Like a few other things in this book, this might counter what you've heard, read or even been taught by other LinkedIn trainers.

The reason I know this to be fact and not opinion is two-fold. 1. I've heard from hundreds of people, including high-level decision-makers, that they HATE it when they get a personalised connection request on LinkedIn, and it often puts them off from accepting. 2. Having sent thousands of connection requests over the years, the majority have not been personalised and nearly always accepted.

There is a time when personalising your connection request is beneficial. . .

This is when you're trying to connect with people higher up in a company's hierarchy—Directors, C-Level, Owners, etc. Senior business leaders do everything they can to shield themselves from salespeople (which traditionally involves having a PA or assistant to manage their phone calls). On LinkedIn, they have full control and are sometimes hesitant to connect with every salesperson who sends a request (as many then receive a spammy sales pitch straight after accepting!).

This is why adding a note is important for these decision-makers because they will need a reason to accept your request.

BONUS TIP: If you're trying to connect with someone very high up in a company, I recommend connecting first with other people in the business. As a potential second step, you could also engage on some of their and their company's LinkedIn page posts. This makes you visible, and when you send the decision-maker a connection request, they'll see that you're already connected with several people at the company, making you seem warmer.

For many other people that you want to connect with, I'd recommend not adding a note and simply sending the request as it is.

AFTER THEY ACCEPT. . .

For the ones that you do send a personalised connection request, if they do accept, which hopefully they will, you're then faced with a tricky situation. Most people (9 out of 10) won't reply to your personalised note, which is now technically the first message of the conversation! So, you will need to send another message, even though this will feel more like the first message that you sent.

For this situation, I personally recommend that the message you send is either audio or video (you'll learn all about those in this book) so that you're not following a written message with another written message.

PART 1
PROSPECTING WITH MESSAGES

CHAPTER 1

MOTIVATION TO MESSAGE

If there is one thing that I have experienced consistently with messaging on LinkedIn during my time as a sales leader and over the last seven years training companies and sales teams across the world, it's that a lot of people are scared to send messages to other people.

Either that or they're simply not sending enough messages. I learned a big lesson very early in my sales career when I was knocking on people's doors, trying to sell TV services. Some days I would have to knock on over 100 doors to try and hit my target for the day. Now, most of those doors didn't answer, and out of those that did, a lot of them slammed the door in my face (some even swearing as they slammed it).

But there would always be at least one person that would answer, listen and then would express an interest. They actually needed the product I was selling, and I was able to help them.

This was where my love of sales was born and where my motivation grew to find people that I could help. What I realised was that there were always people out there who needed whatever product or service I was selling—my job was to find them.

When it comes to messaging, my mantra, and what I've taught salespeople all over the world, is:

> "There are people out there who NEED and WANT what you sell. They're waiting for you to get in touch with them and show them how you can help them. It all starts with a message."

> "Each message to a prospect could be the message that leads you to your NEXT big sale."

> "The worst that can happen is that they're not interested right now—the best that can happen is that they are."

To everyone reading this book, my hope is that it not only shows you how to send super-effective messages on LinkedIn, but also motivates you to send more. Reaching out to more prospects, starting more conversations, and by doing so, helping you, your teams and your companies sell more.

If you believe you can help someone with your product or service, message them.

Don't wait around.

Don't wait for your competitors to message them first.

Don't wait for them to come to you when they're ready.

They might need what you sell without realising it. Message them, start the conversation and show them that you can help.

CHAPTER 2

THE PROSPECTING MAZE

Not that long ago, salespeople only had a few methods to contact prospects and customers. They could pick up the phone and call them, send them a letter, perhaps even send them a fax or see them face to face.

As time has gone on, technology has advanced, and we now live in a time where there have never been more platforms for communication.

Suddenly, we have text, email, social media, video and more. As salespeople we must realise that our prospects are all using these different methods, and we now have more chances than ever to reach them. What an exciting time to be working in sales, right?!

Never before has a salesperson had SO MANY selling tools available. Yes, it means we have more to learn and master, but it creates so many more opportunities to sell.

Due to the variety of available communication platforms, we all might prefer to use different ones. Some people prefer the phone, some prefer social media and some prefer email.

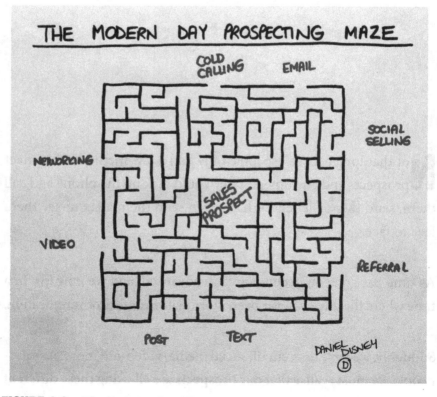

FIGURE 1.1 The Prospecting Maze

There's no right or wrong here, just individual choice. And this is the reality of prospecting, of modern-day digital prospecting. It involves multiple channels, multiple platforms and tools, but what that creates is multiple opportunities to reach and engage your prospects and customers.

I think one of the best ways to illustrate it is to use a finger maze puzzle. . .

You might have seen one of these maze puzzles before. Several doors go into the maze, but only one will lead to the end in the middle. You follow different paths with your finger or a pen to try and get it right.

Now, in our modern-day world, each of our prospects and customers sits in their own little maze. Even you, the reader, as a consumer and buyer, will sit in your own little maze.

Each door into the maze represents a method of communication. One door represents the phone or cold calling, one door represents email, one social media, one face-to-face—you get the idea. As we all know with these puzzles, only one (or two) doors will lead to the middle, and in the modern-day prospecting maze, often only one or two doors will lead you to the prospect (Figure 1.1).

And this is what I call the modern-day prospecting maze!

Now this is the important part. . .

EVERYONE IS DIFFERENT! Each maze around each individual prospect is different. For some prospects, the door that gets you to the prospect in the middle is the phone. For some prospects, the door that gets you to the prospect in the middle is via email. For some, it will be social media.

And this is the crucial reality for sellers today. We have never had as many communication tools, and they will probably only continue to grow. Thirty years ago, the prospecting maze consisted of far fewer doors, making it a lot simpler to reach prospects. It was also easier for prospects to ignore us.

There are many more doors now, which, on the one hand, makes it more complicated but, on the other hand, means as a salesperson, you've got MORE opportunities to reach prospects.

Let me give you an example. . .

Let's say that I am a prospect, and you are trying to sell to me (which many people have done over the years and continue to do on a daily basis).

If you were to go through the cold calling door in my prospecting maze (in other words, use cold calling to try and sell to me), you would end up at a dead end.

Personally, I don't answer cold calls, even though I've spent years making them and years training and leading salespeople making them. As a buyer, it's not a method that I personally respond to. It doesn't matter how many times you try to call me; I won't answer.

I'm not alone with this; there are many people around the world, likely including many of YOUR prospects, who don't and will never answer cold calls.

The reason this point is so important is that there are still many companies out there where their ONLY prospecting method is cold calling. There are also companies where cold calling is the core method alongside email. If this is you or your company, you're missing out on all of the prospects you could reach and sell to if you were to use other methods, such as LinkedIn and Social Selling.

As a salesperson, if you REALLY want to sell to me, let's say I am a huge prospect for you and one that you are confident you can help, you need to do something different.

Perhaps you'll connect with me via email, or perhaps you'll see me at an event, but what will increase your chances is to connect and engage with me via LinkedIn.

This is the reality of sales. If you're restricting yourself to just one or two methods, you're simply limiting yourself. Some of your prospects will NEVER answer a cold call. Some will NEVER reply to your email. Some will ONLY talk to you if you engage with them effectively via LinkedIn or social media.

NOTE: I'm not saying one is better than the other—I want this message to be clear.

To reach the maximum number of prospects, you need to use ALL of the available tools. Some prospects will only ever talk to you via the phone. However, it's important to appreciate that there is a percentage of your prospects that prefer digital communication.

In this book, I will show you one of the many ways you can leverage LinkedIn and social media for selling. LinkedIn messages are a tremendously powerful tool when used right—trust me, I've created and closed loads of B2B deals through LinkedIn messages.

The "Modern Day Prospecting Maze" is there to help you understand the prospecting landscape that is out there now.

The most effective sellers use as many of the available doors as possible to increase their chances of reaching the prospect in the middle.

> "If you sit around and wait for customers to come to you, you risk losing them to your competitors who don't sit and wait. They make contact first."

CHAPTER 3

OUTBOUND SOCIAL SELLING

O ver the last few years, I've noticed one thing...

A lot, and I mean A LOT, of salespeople, sales leaders, and even sales experts only think of social selling as an <u>INBOUND</u>-generating activity. They see it as sharing content to generate inbound leads.

Whilst it is, of course, a very powerful inbound lead-generating platform, it is equally a very powerful <u>OUTBOUND</u>-lead-generating platform.

For those who may not be familiar with these terms, inbound leads are leads that come into you. For example, someone visits your LinkedIn profile or reads content that you've shared and then sends YOU a message enquiring about your product or service. That is seen as an inbound lead.

Inbound leads are more commonly generated by marketing departments, where they are then sometimes qualified and passed on to the sales department.

Outbound leads are more commonly generated by salespeople via prospecting activities where they go out and generate the opportunity. For example, cold calling will find salespeople phone up totally cold prospects and work to turn them into sales opportunities. They have gone out and created an opportunity from nothing.

Right now, one of the biggest missed opportunities in sales is generating more outbound social selling opportunities.

Let me show you what I mean. . .

Say you're a B2B sales rep, and as part of a social selling push, you write an article on LinkedIn. After that article goes out and gets some good engagement, a nice little message pops up in your LinkedIn message inbox from a prospect saying they liked your blog and would like more information or the opportunity to discuss the product or service you sell.

That would be an inbound lead.

I don't think many people out there would disagree with me here.

This is where the argument is often based that social selling is in fact not selling but social marketing.

Based on that example alone, I would agree.

If you're creating content and then waiting for inbound leads to come in, that is simply a marketing activity.

Now let's say you wrote and published that article on LinkedIn. Perhaps you had a few inbound enquiries come through, which is great.

But let's say that you then decided to look at the engagement—the likes, comments and shares.

Whilst sifting through those engagements, you notice that someone who works within one of your prospect companies had actually clicked 'like' on your blog.

If you then connect with them and send them a message to start a conversation, this is where <u>OUTBOUND</u> social selling comes in. This is where you are starting the conversation, not waiting for them to start it.

I'll share a real example of this:

Many years ago, whilst selling in the IT industry and trying to reach IT Managers/IT Directors, there was one company in particular that I was struggling to get through to.

They were a medium-sized business, around 200+ staff, and I could not get through to the decision-maker via cold calling or email. I had been trying to reach them for around two months.

One day, I published an article on LinkedIn. It wasn't an article based on the IT industry, so it wasn't aimed at my target prospects. Instead, it was an article on sales, the subject I knew I could more effectively write about. When looking at the engagement, I noticed that a sales rep from within the company I was trying to prospect had clicked 'like' on my blog.

TOP TIP: *When you create and share content on LinkedIn, whether it's a blog, post, video, photo, etc., you can't see the people who "view" the content. You could get 1,000 views, but you'll never be able to see who they are.*

When they engage with the content, such as clicking "like," commenting or sharing the content, THAT'S when you can actually see them.

Once you can see them, you can then connect with them and use it to start a conversation. This is why I encourage everyone to create content on LinkedIn with the goal of generating sales and clients to drive as much engagement to their content as possible.

It's only through the engagement that you can actually see who is engaging and start talking to them.

After realising that this sales rep had clicked *"like,"* I knew I had an opportunity to find a different route to my target decision-maker.

I connected with the sales rep and sent them a nice, simple conversational message (which you'll also find in the template chapter later on in this book):

> *Hi John,*
>
> *Thank you for clicking like on my article! I hope you enjoyed it; I'd love to know what your thoughts were on the subject?*
>
> *Kind regards,*
> *Dan*

They replied straight away, and we started chatting. I didn't jump in trying to pitch them, nor did I jump in straight away asking for the phone number of their IT Director. Instead, I talked to them about the subject of the article that they liked.

We sent a few messages back and forth, building a nice bit of rapport, where I had then earned the opportunity to discuss what I was selling.

I then mentioned that I had actually been trying to reach their IT Director to discuss what I was selling. They were more than happy to make an introduction and actually went on to arrange a phone call for me with them.

After that phone call, I was then able to progress it into a meeting and eventually go on to win that sale.

I would argue very strongly that it is outbound selling. It's no different from cold calling someone; you are sending someone a message who doesn't necessarily know you with the aim of creating a sales opportunity.

Just like a cold call, some won't reply/answer, and some will. The ones who do reply can then be groomed, turning into real sales opportunities.

It's time to start using social selling for both inbound AND outbound selling!

In my experience, most salespeople are either sending terrible sales pitch messages OR just not using social media in any way to generate outbound opportunities.

LinkedIn messaging is one of the most powerful ways you can leverage Social Selling. I believe it is absolutely no different from cold calling.

In many ways, it can be a much warmer version, with the opportunity for already having connected with them, built credibility and trust, and started building rapport.

PART 2
RESEARCH & PERSONALISATION

CHAPTER 4

WHY AREN'T PEOPLE REPLYING?

You've found your prospect on LinkedIn and sent them a well-crafted LinkedIn message, but then something unexpected happens. . .

They don't reply.

Come to think of it, not many of your prospects are replying to your LinkedIn messages. . . What's going on?!

Let me share with you the three most likely reasons people aren't replying to your LinkedIn messages (and what you can do to get them to reply):

NUMBER 1 – YOU DIDN'T PERSONALISE THE MESSAGE!

The number of messages that I get (and have seen decision-makers get) have ZERO personalisation. . . On occasion, they might add your name in, but that's about it.

If the message is more about YOU than it is about them, you're unlikely to get a reply. One of the easiest and quickest changes you can make to your social selling process is to make more of your messaging about THEM.

- Not about your company but about theirs
- Not about your product but what it will do for them
- Not about you but about them

Before you write your message, do your homework. Look through their LinkedIn profile, search through their recent LinkedIn activity, look at their company's page on LinkedIn, and if you're still struggling to find good usable information, look at other people working at their company; there is always someone sharing good insights.

NUMBER 2 – THEY HAVE NO IDEA WHO YOU ARE!

A lot of LinkedIn messages go unanswered because they're just too cold. The prospect is looking at this message thinking. . .

The beauty of LinkedIn and social selling is that your messages don't actually need to be cold, and there are a few things you can do before messaging (that will only take a few days) to warm them up, increasing the response rate.

Step One: Engage on a few of the posts that they're sharing on LinkedIn. Click '*like*' and then write a nice CONTRIBUTING comment. This does not mean a "Great post, Sarah!" comment but something more tangible like, "Really enjoyed this post, Sarah. A similar thing actually happened to me a few years back. . ." A good comment may even get a reply from them and beginning a conversation.

Step Two: Connect with other people in the company and engage on their posts as well. The decision-maker will likely notice this, further warming up their relationship with you (before you've even spoken directly).

Step Three: Share your own content during this time as well so they're getting value from you and getting to know you. Make sure the content is industry-relevant and valuable to them to make the right impact.

NUMBER 3 – YOU'RE ONLY SENDING TEXT-BASED MESSAGES

As of this writing, I would say around 99% of the messages in my LinkedIn inbox are text-based written messages. From the conversations I have with leaders all over the world, it's the same for them. This means that if you're only sending written messages, it's just another written message in a huge pile of other written messages. . .

If you want to stand out, capture their attention and increase your chances of a reply, it might be time to get more creative.

Utilise the two other ways that you can send messages on LinkedIn right now, audio voice notes and video messages. Not only do they stand out because so few are using them, but they allow you to take your message to the next level, adding in voice/tone and even body language/eye contact.

Audio/Voice Notes – Keep it short and sweet, around 30–60 seconds. Make it as much about them as possible and have a simple CTA (call to action) for their response.

Video Messages – You can send a maximum of two minutes, although 60–90 seconds is optimal. Look at the camera for good eye contact and be aware of lighting, what you're wearing and what's behind you in the camera shot.

There it is. . .

Three of the most common reasons why your prospects are likely not replying to your LinkedIn messages. Hopefully some of these tips will help you generate more replies, and from those replies, more pipeline and sales!

"The more you make your message about them, the more likely they will be to reply to you."

CHAPTER 5

RESEARCH, PERSONALISATION & RELEVANCE

There's an essential formula that I teach when it comes to messaging on LinkedIn, and it's this:

R + P X R = REPLIES

Research + Personalisation × Relevance = Replies

When I scroll through my LinkedIn inbox, looking at the messages I get from salespeople trying to sell me something, there is one thing that most of them have in common:

Nothing in the message is about me, the prospect.

It's all about them. Who THEY are, what THEY are selling, what THEIR company does, what THEIR product does, etc. This spray-and-pray approach doesn't work (I'm not sure if or when it ever did); ultimately, it is lazy selling. Create a template, copy and paste it, and send it to as many people as possible to see if someone bites. It's lazy, and not only does it rarely (if ever) yield results, but you also run the risk of giving potential prospects an incredibly poor first impression of you.

This is why personalisation is so important and why good research is crucial to find the information you need to personalise the message properly.

It's no longer enough to scrape their name, position and company name from LinkedIn. You need to dig deeper. The deeper you dig, and the more relevant you make the message, the more impact it will have.

How much research should I do? How LONG should I spend researching someone?

This is very important:

The amount of time that you spend researching a prospect should be reflective of the potential value of their business for you.

The bigger the potential value of the sale, the more research you should do. If it's a small, low-value opportunity, then you shouldn't spend as much time on it. You don't want to waste time extensively researching one individual prospect that becomes a low-value sale and holds you up from the time you should have been spending prospecting to more people.

WHERE TO RESEARCH?

This is the exciting part—LinkedIn is literally a GOLD MINE of information. You can look at it like layers that you dig through, and the deeper you dig, the more valuable the prospect is potentially. Here are the layers/different places you can research prospects:

LAYER 1 – BASIC RESEARCHING

LinkedIn Profile & LinkedIn Activity

The first step is to read through their LinkedIn profile. Look at the summary section, look at their employment history, look at who has given them recommendations, look at what pages and groups they follow. There is a lot of information that can be used just from their LinkedIn profile.

You can then go into their LinkedIn activity. You can look at all the content they have posted. If they're actively posting content, this is a great opportunity to engage on the post (click 'like' and add a comment) and then use the post to start a conversation (there are templates for this later in the chapter). You can also see the content that THEY are engaging on (liking and commenting). This can give you insights into subjects and topics they're interested in and industry influencers they might follow and respond to. You can also see any articles they have written and published as well as any PDF carousels or slideshows that they've shared.

LAYER 2 – DEEPER RESEARCH

LinkedIn Company Page & Activity

To go a level deeper, you can then go to their LinkedIn company page, which will include some basic information and usually a link through to their website.

What you'll also be able to see and look through is their company's LinkedIn activity and all the content that they have been posting. This can be full of insights and information that are worth using, such as company announcements.

LAYER 3 – ADVANCED RESEARCH

Other Employees' Profiles & Activity

The final layer can often contain the largest quantity of information and also present multiple alternative routes into the company.

When you're on their LinkedIn company's page, you'll be able to see a list of all the employees' profiles at that company.

This will include other decision-makers as well as people within their own team and other teams in the business. Some of these people might have more relevant and valuable information in their profile and through their activity. Some of them will be more active, posting more content and, therefore, giving you more insight into the company.

If you're selling to a CMO, for example, looking through the rest of the marketing team can be valuable. If you're struggling to get a response from the CMO, sending a message to the marketing manager, supervisor or anyone else on the team can sometimes get you a foot in the door.

Then there are other departments that you can tap into. I can't count the number of times I've made contact with the sales department of a company where I was ultimately trying to sell to the CTO.

WHAT TO RESEARCH

The next question is: What are you looking for? What information is actually going to be valuable in the message?

If your personalisation isn't authentic, it won't work. You can spend hours researching someone, but if you then present it in a sales-y way, it won't work.

The key is to look for *CONVERSATION STARTING* opportunities. You'll find a lot of these throughout the templates included in this book, but here are some to give you an idea:

Their Company – Have you worked with them before? Are you working with a similar company? Do you know someone who works there?

Their Summary – What have they done before that you might have a connection or experience with? What do they do now that you have a connection with?

Their Activity – What have they done recently? What has their company done recently? What are they interested in or passionate about?

The CEO – What are they sharing on LinkedIn? What information is on their profile? What announcements have they made recently?

Their Colleagues – Who is the most active on LinkedIn? What are they sharing? What insights do they have?

"In sales, there is a fine balance between persistence and pestering. The best salespeople know how to be persistent without pestering their prospects."

CHAPTER 6

THE ONE THING TO AVOID

Recently, a salesperson asked for my help on a particular prospect they were pursuing. They had tried "everything" and couldn't get a response from this prospect.

To try and figure out what might be blocking this potential opportunity, I asked them to show me their LinkedIn inbox and the message they had sent.

What I saw shocked me. . .

It wasn't the first time I'd seen this happen, but it was one of the worst cases I'd ever witnessed. It was the ONE thing you must try to avoid when sending messages on LinkedIn.

Let me just set the scene so you can understand why this was such a big problem:

You must have seen that scene in a film or series where there is a crazy significant other who is perhaps a little *too* keen.

Their partner gets home and checks their house phone expecting 1 or 2 voicemails. This is where it usually states:

"You have. . . 100 messages."

They might go something like this:

"Hey, Chris, it's Sarah here. I had a great time yesterday. Call me when you get home."

"Hey, Chris, Sarah again. Just thought I'd check if you were home yet. Call me."

"Just making sure you're okay, Chris. Call me as soon as you get this."

"Did you just try and call? My phone went off, but I didn't see who it was. Call me."

"Did I do something wrong, Chris? Why are you ignoring me?"

"I'm sorry for the last message. I'm just worried about you. Call me."

You're probably getting where I'm going with this, but it's happening in sales, and it's happening on LinkedIn. Message trails that look something like this:

"Hi, Jane, my name is Daniel, and I work for Software King. Our product does lots of amazing things, and we are a really amazing company. I'd love to chat and see how we could work together. Here is a link to my calendar so you can book a meeting with me."

"Hey, Jane. Just wanted to see if you'd received my last message?"

"Hi, Jane. Here's a testimonial from one of our customers! Are you free tomorrow for a chat?"

"Jane, not sure if you're getting my messages. Could you let me know if you can see these?"

It's crazy to think people do this and think it will work, but they do. Going back to the salesperson I was telling you about, well. . . They had sent EIGHT MESSAGES to a prospect with zero replies. Each message got worse and worse.

Imagine if a salesperson messaged YOU eight times trying to sell to you. Would you reply? Probably not.

And so, this is the ONE thing to avoid above all others. . .

If you've sent a message and they haven't replied, don't try the same type of message again. Don't worry if you've already done this, by the way. It's never too late to turn it around.

> *"Okay, Dan, we get that this probably doesn't look great and won't work, but then what is it that we COULD do instead?"*

Let's say you've sent a written prospecting message to someone and they haven't replied. I'd encourage you to first wait 5–7 days for a reply, and if nothing comes back, then your next step should be to try a DIFFERENT TYPE of message. If your first message was a text-based written message, then your best options to follow up are either an AUDIO or VIDEO message.

Not only is this a pattern interruption to what they'll be used to, but you also increase your chance of getting a response by utilising different forms of communication. Plus, it will look a lot better compared to multiple written messages.

When you send an audio message, it shows up as a volume bar with a play button, and when you send a video, it shows up as an image with a play button, so they'll all look completely different.

> "No one wakes up in the morning and hopes that they receive a terrible, spammy, non-personalised sales pitch message in their inbox."

CHAPTER 7

NO ONE LIKES SPAM MESSAGES

THIS IS VERY IMPORTANT! PLEASE READ!

In this book, I'm going to show you how one single LinkedIn message opened the door to a sale worth over £1,000,000.

What I need you to know and remember is that this was a 100% personal and individual message, not a spam one sent out to hundreds or thousands of prospects. This message template, and the others included in this book, will work best if you send them to qualified prospects on an individual basis.

Spam selling really isn't a strong strategy in sales anymore. Copying and pasting generic messages and sending them to all of your connections on LinkedIn will struggle to yield a positive response. What *does* work is sending personalised messages to relevant people.

NO ONE LIKES SPAM!

I'm sure you don't like receiving spam messages. I bet even the people SENDING the spam messages don't like receiving them!

Yet I would bet that 80–90% of the LinkedIn messages sent right now are considered spammy messages. (Spammy messages are sales messages sent to prospects who don't need or want your product or service, often in an aggressive or sleazy sales style.)

Please, when reading this book and using these templates, make sure you understand that I only ever approach prospects with these message templates that I have qualified myself and am confident I can help.

Not only will you save time from sending hundreds of wasted messages, but you'll also increase your chances of conversion and success.

Let me share with you some of the messages that I get on a regular basis in my LinkedIn inbox! I won't share who they are from—that would just be mean!

EXAMPLES

My inbox is filled with LinkedIn messages daily, and unfortunately, 80% of them are terrible (another motivation behind writing this book!).

But if you read these and know deep down that you've sent similar ones, hopefully this will be an eye-opener. . .

The WAY TOO LONG Message

I had to cut this up into three sections to be able to fit it into one single slide; it was WAY too long! You can tell it's been copied and pasted from an email, which is not a strategy I would ever recommend.

LinkedIn messaging is more of an instant messaging platform than an email platform. It's designed for short, conversational messages. You'll see as you read through this book that these light, conversation-starting messages work so much better than copy-and-pasted emails like Figure 7.1.

Keep them short, keep them valuable and keep them conversational.

However, they can get a little too short sometimes. . .

So, whilst this example was of a message that was way too long, here are a couple of examples of messages that I've received that are way too short:

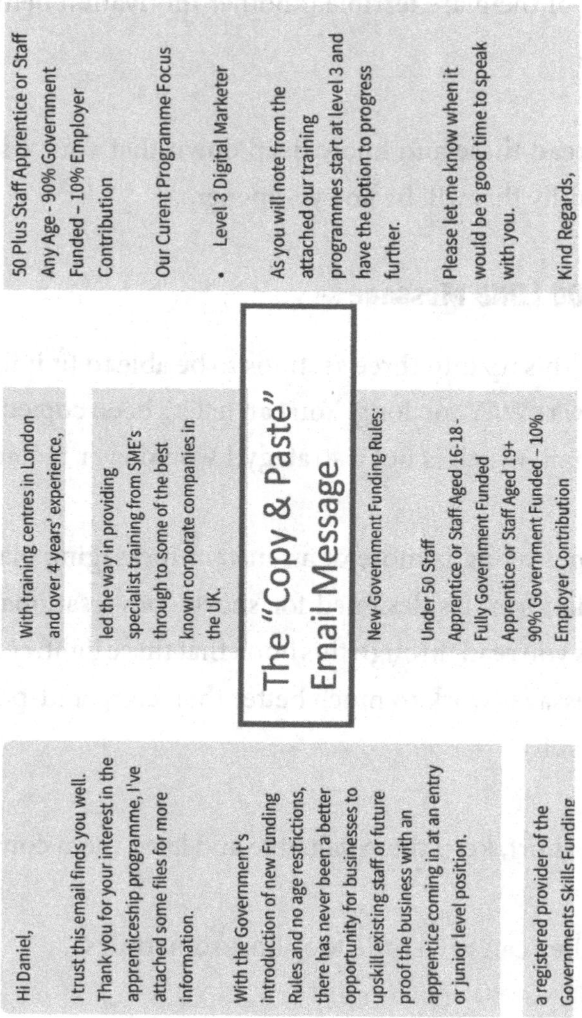

Hi Daniel,

I trust this email finds you well. Thank you for your interest in the apprenticeship programme, I've attached some files for more information.

With the Government's introduction of new Funding Rules and no age restrictions, there has never been a better opportunity for businesses to upskill existing staff or future proof the business with an apprentice coming in at an entry or junior level position.

a registered provider of the Governments Skills Funding

With training centres in London and over 4 years' experience,

led the way in providing specialist training from SME's through to some of the best known corporate companies in the UK.

New Government Funding Rules:

Under 50 Staff
Apprentice or Staff Aged 16-18 - Fully Government Funded
Apprentice or Staff Aged 19+ 90% Government Funded – 10% Employer Contribution

50 Plus Staff Apprentice or Staff Any Age - 90% Government Funded – 10% Employer Contribution

Our Curent Programme Focus

- Level 3 Digital Marketer

As you will note from the attached our training programmes start at level 3 and have the option to progress further.

Please let me know when it would be a good time to speak with you.

Kind Regards,

The "Copy & Paste" Email Message

FIGURE 7.1   The Way Too Long Message

The Way Too Short Message

I also get messages that simply just say, "Hi!" Again, not a strategy I recommend if you actually want to generate results from LinkedIn and Social Selling. In fact, I don't think I even send my friends messages like this, let alone prospects or customers.

Whilst LinkedIn messaging is a more instant-message conversational style platform, the Figure 7.2 example is perhaps a little too extreme.

There are a few other examples of messages that are perhaps a little too chatty or too needy. . .

I must add that I don't know any of these people, have never spoken with them, and that this is their first communication with me. It was their approach to starting a conversation with me, and, unfortunately, not a successful attempt.

These examples were my motivation to write this book. My inbox (like many others out there) is filled DAILY with messages like these or very sales-driven messages.

Unfortunately, the majority of sales-driven messages are selling a product that I have no need for at all. Worst yet, the salesperson sending them could have found that out had they spent just one minute looking at my LinkedIn profile.

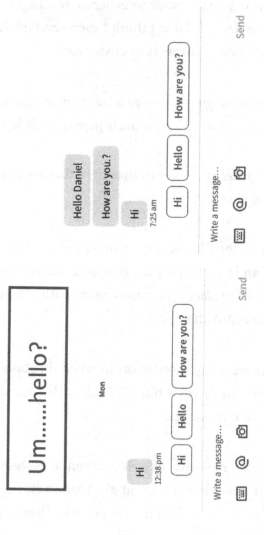

FIGURE 7.2 The Way Too Short Message

There is one more bad message style that is currently one of the worst out there. . .

I believe it's a style that has unfortunately been taught by some of the other LinkedIn/Social Selling experts, but it is one that is hated by decision-makers and one that I find quite shocking.

It gives the impression that you value YOUR time above theirs, which isn't something I would personally recommend. . .

The "Here's MY Calendar Link" Message

This is the "Here is MY calendar link for YOU to book a meeting with me" message. It's one of the most ego-driven examples of selling I've seen in modern-day sales. It's very much like the cheesy, sleazy salespeople of the past (Figure 7.3).

It suggests that your time is more valuable and important than the time of your prospects, which isn't a great way to present yourself when trying to win business.

Don't get me wrong; online calendars are great! They're super-efficient and effective in booking meetings with prospects and customers.

As a salesperson, you need to EARN the right to a conversation, demo or meeting.

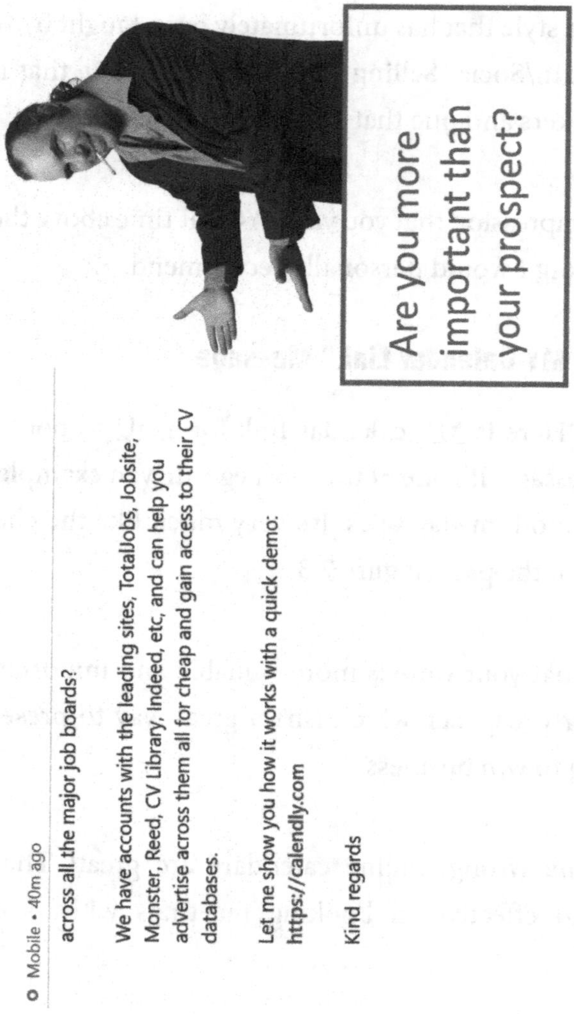

Mobile · 40m ago

across all the major job boards?

We have accounts with the leading sites, TotalJobs, Jobsite, Monster, Reed, CV Library, Indeed, etc, and can help you advertise across them all for cheap and gain access to their CV databases.

Let me show you how it works with a quick demo:
https://calendly.com

Kind regards

Are you more important than your prospect?

FIGURE 7.3 The Calendar Link

After you've given value, built a relationship and qualified them as a prospect, then is the time to ask THEM if they would be happy to arrange a phone call or face-to-face meeting.

If they are happy, then you can send them a link to your calendar. Even then, though, I still recommend asking them what dates/times work best for them. The sheer act of sending them your calendar link places value on your own time above them.

Only if you've gone back and forth a few times and are struggling to find a date that works for both of you does the online calendar link truly provide value in sales.

TO PITCH OR NOT TO PITCH?

That is the question—and a big question when it comes to messaging on LinkedIn. There is a lot of negative content around sending pitches on LinkedIn, BUT there are actually two types of LinkedIn pitch messages, and one of them actually works.

You see, the problem is that most people, when sending sales pitch–style messages on LinkedIn, send non-personalised spammy pitches. Those definitely don't work. Ever. However, there is a type of pitch message that does work, which I'll share here and which you'll see in some of the templates in this book.

The first question you have when sending a message on LinkedIn is whether you should start a conversation or send a sales pitch. There are a few variables that will impact your answer when choosing which to use for a prospective customer:

1) How senior they are in the company
2) How active they are on LinkedIn
3) What size the potential opportunity might be
4) What size the company is

Let's just accept something for a minute that is counterintuitive to 99% of the content you see on LinkedIn right now...

Some people actually PREFER getting pitched on LinkedIn. True story.

Why? Because they don't want the "fake" dance salespeople often do when they're only looking to sell something. They just want you to tell them what you think you can do for them, and if it's something they see value in, they'll entertain it.

In my personal experience, I've found this to be more the case with senior decision-makers, C-Level execs, VPs, owners, founders, etc. These are some of the busiest people you'll sell to, and you'll be far more successful getting to the point than trying to lure them into a fluffy conversation they simply don't have time for. It's often the same with people who aren't very active on LinkedIn, are not posting or engaging a lot, and often with networks below 1,000 connections/followers.

The KEY, and something you'll see throughout this book, is when you use a straight-to-pitch approach, make the pitch about THEM and not about you. It's not about you and your product, it's about their problems and your solution. It's about how THEY will benefit and what they gain from the opportunity.

On the flipside, you then have people that DO want the conversation. They don't want you to just jump in with the pitch; they would much rather get to know you first and build some level of rapport.

People in mid-management and below, those who are much more active on LinkedIn, and those with larger audiences tend to be more responsive to conversation-starting messages.

PART 3
LINKEDIN MESSAGING THOUGHTS

CHAPTER 8

INMAIL VERSUS MESSAGE

For those of you who aren't sure of the difference between a LinkedIn InMail and a LinkedIn message, allow me to clarify it for you.

A LinkedIn message is a message you send to a direct connection on LinkedIn. Someone who you have connected with, they have accepted, and they are now a 1st-degree connection.

NOTE: If you are only "Following" them on LinkedIn, whilst you will be able to see their activity, you will not be able to message them directly. This is only possible when you are connected with someone.

A LinkedIn InMail is a message sent to someone that you are NOT connected with. You can only send these with LinkedIn Premium or LinkedIn Sales Navigator.

My recommendation has been and always will be to try and connect with a prospect first and then send them a LinkedIn message. The conversion and success rates are incredibly higher with LinkedIn messages compared to InMails.

THAT BEING SAID. . .

Some people won't accept your connection request. It doesn't matter how great your personal brand might be or your personalised connection request, some prospects and decision-makers simply won't accept. In those instances, InMail is one of your only options and, when done right, can still prove to be very effective.

If you can, try to connect with your prospect or target customer first and then send a LinkedIn message. If after 7–14 days they haven't accepted your connection request, then look at utilising InMail instead.

If you are a Sales Navigator user, you'll benefit from Chapter 21, "InMail Messages on LinkedIn," where I go through all of the processes and strategies, along with templates, to help you turn your InMails into opportunities.

"There is no one-size-fits-all in sales. Different prospects respond to different approaches. Your role as a sales professional is to adapt to each potential customer."

CHAPTER 9

WHEN TO SEND A MESSAGE ON LINKEDIN

Timing is very important when it comes to sending messages on LinkedIn; we've all seen the memes showing someone disappointed with the text, "That moment you accept a connection request and then instantly get hit with a sales pitch."

Some call it spray and pray.
Some call it spamming.
Some call it pitch slapping.

It actually can get worse than that. . .

Some people now connect and then send a really nice, well-written and personalised message. "What's wrong with that, Dan?" I hear you ask. . .

Well, this is what usually happens:

SALESPERSON: "Hi, Dan, I really loved your post last week. Thank you for connecting. Was the sales manager you mentioned really that bad?"

ME: "Ah, thank you. I'm glad you like the post. Yes, they really were. It's scary to think there are managers out there like that."

SALESPERSON: "Yes, I agree. By the way, I saw you're the CEO of *The Daily Sales,* and I wondered if you were free tomorrow to discuss a new email platform for your business?"

Insert Ron Burgandy saying, "*Well, that escalated quickly*" (an Anchorman reference for anyone who didn't get it).

So, when I say timing is important, it's really important.

There are a few factors that will determine the best time to message a prospect. Some prospects are best messaged quite soon after connecting, such as C-Level, VPs and senior leadership roles. They are often too busy to do the social selling "dance" of engagement and content sharing and often prefer that you just message them with what you offer. There are several templates in this book that show you the right way to do this.

Then you get mid-level management positions and lower; they usually are more responsive when you take a little time. Do more research and do some social engagement beforehand.

Here are my recommended timings:

Senior Leadership & C-Level: 1–2 days after connecting

Mid-Level Management: 3–4 days after connecting (and after engagement)

Large/Enterprise Accounts: 1–2 weeks after connecting (and after extensive research and account mapping)

CHAPTER 10

ONE SIZE DOESN'T FIT ALL

Before we dig into the multi-million message, I need you to understand that one size doesn't fit all.

This is the same for cold calls, for sales emails, and for face-to-face meetings. If you take one approach and apply it to every prospect you try and sell to, you'll rarely succeed.

Each of your prospects is an individual, different in their own unique ways. One of the most important skills a salesperson can possess is the ability to adapt and mirror their prospects and customers. This is the same rule with Social Selling; it's important to treat each prospect as an individual.

Sales work best when you stop trying to sell to anyone and everyone and start selling to the people who actually need what you sell.

Whilst the core message in *The Ultimate LinkedIn Messaging Guide* may have unlocked a huge sale for me, it doesn't mean you can copy it, paste it, send it to every single one of your prospects and expect the sales will start flooding in!

Different prospects, different products and different industries will all play a role in the type of messaging you want to use on LinkedIn.

Therefore, I didn't just want to share the multi-million message with you; I wanted to provide you with as many proven LinkedIn message templates as possible.

After I take you through the story of the multi-million LinkedIn message, I'm going to share 25 tried, tested and proven LinkedIn messages.

Each template includes notes that will hopefully help you determine which of your prospects might benefit from it and how best to use it.

I'd then highly recommend finding the templates that suit each individual prospect. It may be challenging at first, but as with anything, once you learn and practice it, it soon becomes routine.

Now, after many years of sending LinkedIn messages, I know very quickly which template works best for each new prospect I approach.

> *"There are people out there right now who need what you are selling but have no idea who you are. Each prospecting message that you send has the chance of reaching one of those people."*

PART 4
WRITTEN LINKEDIN MESSAGES

CHAPTER 11

THE SEVEN-FIGURE LINKEDIN MESSAGE

Here is the whole story of how a single individual LinkedIn message opened the door to one of the biggest sales in my career.

I will go into as much detail as I can as the processes completed before and after the message are equally as important as the message itself.

Setting the scene

Whilst working for a large IT company in the UK, my team mainly sold IT training packages to SMEs (small to medium-sized employers).

When selling to SMEs, it's often very easy to reach decision-makers via cold calling—well, it certainly used to be back then—as there aren't as many people or layers in the business.

We would go in and present a variety of training packages valued between £3,000 and £18,000. The sales process often took around 1–2 months from prospecting through to closing.

Most of the time, we would first cold-call to find the decision-maker and aim to either email information over or book a meeting straight off the call.

During the meeting, we would then run through needs, listen and learn about the prospect. After that, we would go back, put together a proposal and call or meet them again to run through it.

It was a highly competitive market; we had a lot of competitors, some bigger and some cheaper than us. A lot of our success came down to either being the first to contact the prospect or our ability to build stronger relationships.

Following some really rapid growth, and as the top-performing person in sales, I was tasked with bringing new, large corporate clients to our portfolio. I very quickly found that cold calling was not as effective as it was with smaller companies!

Complex organisational structures and good gatekeepers made it difficult to get in front of the decision-maker. I learned how to do it effectively, but some companies were extremely challenging.

I was working on a few companies—global companies with multi-billion pound turnover. After, once again, getting stuck at the gate-keeper on a cold call, I decided to look for other ways in. One thing popped into my head: *I wonder if the decision-maker is on LinkedIn?*

I didn't have the name of the decision-maker, only a few job titles that I was currently working with. I was looking for HR Managers, L&D Managers and IT Managers (and above).

After a quick search, there they were! I popped onto their profile, had a read and soon qualified that this was the person I needed and wanted to speak to.

Let me just pause this story for a minute whilst I talk you through this stage:

The first step is to connect with your prospect.

LinkedIn InMails are okay, but they're no different (in some ways worse) than a cold call. When you connect with someone, you are able to send them a LinkedIn message directly, which is far more effective compared to an InMail, which is sent to someone you aren't connected with.

Similar to most of the messages I get, most InMails are even MORE sales-y.

To be able to send a direct message, you need to connect with them first.

When you go on their profile, if they're a 2nd-degree connection, you'll see the option to "Connect." It's a nice blue button just under their LinkedIn banner.

> NOTE: If they're a 3rd-degree connection, you won't see the "Connect" button but instead will see a "Message" button with a little lock image next to it. This means you can only message them via InMails if you have LinkedIn Premium or LinkedIn Sales Navigator. In the past, there was no way that you could send this person a connection request; however, LinkedIn has changed that now.

If you click the "More. . ." button next to the "Message" button, it will open a section with four options: Share Profile, Save to PDF, Connect and Report/Block.

If you click the "Connect" option, it will be the same as clicking the connect button with a 2nd-degree connection.

When you click on the "Connect" button, it will prompt a little pop-up that will say:

"You can customise this invitation.

LinkedIn members are more likely to accept invitations that include a personal note.

Add note – Send now"

Would you like to customise this request? YES! It can be very helpful, depending on the prospect, to personalise your connection request.

However, personalising can work against you! Not only are there a huge number of people out there that will be more than happy to connect to you without a personalised request, but sometimes personalising it can discourage people from connecting.

I get tonnes of requests daily, and a large percentage of the personalised ones are personalised with a sales pitch! This does not help increase your chances of getting accepted.

From my own experience connecting and messaging hundreds of decision-makers, the higher up or more senior the prospect, the more beneficial personalising will be. The key is NOT to personalise it with a sales message. There are several templates you can use for this. Most of the time, I go with something simple like:

"Hi Sally,

I'd love to connect,

Kind Regards,
Dan"

Simple, personal and in no way presents me as someone who is going to try and sell to them. This isn't a sure-fire, guaranteed way to get them to accept; some people need more than this.

Some will need you to engage with their content a bit first. I judge it by how active THEY are on LinkedIn. If they are quite active and have a large network (over 1,000), that tells me they are going to be quite likely to accept my request.

If they're not very active and have a smaller network, it's more likely that I'll need to build some rapport first.

Back to the story...

In this case, the prospect is active, so I went with the small, simple personalisation. Within 30 minutes, they accepted my request—a great start to the process!

Sometimes, it can be smarter after connecting to engage with their content a bit first or share your own content for them to see. You can do this over a few days or 1–2 weeks+ to build some foundations before you go in to start a conversation. Again, make a judgement on the prospect and also the proposition you are offering.

In this case, I was very confident that this company would need and want the product I was selling (from qualifications I had already gained). The prospect was active on LinkedIn, which showed me that sending a message straight away might work well.

What I have found from experience is that the higher up the chain you're pitching, the more direct you should be. If you're selling to Directors or C-Level positions, it can often work better to just go straight in with a message.

BUT!

Obviously, it needs to be a well-crafted message. . .

And this is where the £1,000,000 LinkedIn message was born.

Remember, this is NOT a sales pitch.

This is not about you listing loads of features and benefits or telling them how amazing your product and company are.

It's not about you trying to jump into bed with them straight away.

It is NOT some spammy message.

It is NOT a copy-and-paste job.

It is a simple message with one simple goal. . .

To start a conversation with a potential customer.

Here it is. . .

> *"Hi Sally,*
>
> *Thank you for connecting! I work for a company called X, who is one of the UK's leading providers of IT Training. I would love to learn a bit more about what you're currently using for that?*
>
> *Kind Regards,*
> *Dan"*

It was that simple.

Before you start to feel underwhelmed by this message, this is the message that opened the door to a sale valued at over £1,000,000. It was this single simple message that did it. Not a cold call, not an email, not a letter, not a text, not a video, not the type of LinkedIn messages I get in my inbox, but this simple message.

In sales, we know simple works best. It's when we overcomplicate things that they often go wrong.

This was a small conversational prospecting message that thanked them for connecting, explained who we are and what we do, and asked them a question about what they may already have in place for that product or service.

As a decision-maker reading this, I'm not overwhelmed by some sort of huge message or something that comes across in an aggressive way.

It makes me think of that particular product or service and whether or not I'm happy with what I've currently got, whether I need it or whether I may want to change it.

Of course, this doesn't work for everyone.

As I mentioned earlier, this isn't something you can just copy and paste a thousand times. However, with the right prospects, this can and does work. For me, on this occasion and for this particular prospect, I received a reply within an hour.

I can actually remember the exact moment; I was having lunch with a colleague (fish and chips with a cold can of lemonade) and decided to check my phone. Logging into LinkedIn, I saw the little notification on the messages, opened it up and was met with a reply.

Let's just say I did a little fist pump in the air when I read the reply and saw there was a potential opportunity brewing right there!

This was the reply I received:

"Hi Dan,

Thank you for your message. This was well-timed as it is some-thing that we've not done before but are actually starting to look at options now. Could you send me some more information about what you offer, please?

Kind Regards,
Sally"

It was a fantastic response; it showed interest and a potential opportunity.

This is another very important part of the process. What do you do next?

Some salespeople will try and send a load of information into another LinkedIn message, which I must advise against! LinkedIn messages are designed to be light and conversational; the moment more detail and information comes into it, it's time to move the conversation away from LinkedIn.

Only in specific situations will the conversation stay on socials, depending on the prospect and the complexity of what it is you're selling.

The information I needed to send was best sent via email—something I still do to this day. My goal next is to try and get an email address with permission to send them information.

I replied:

> "Hi Sally,
>
> That's great to hear. What was the best email address to send the information across to?
>
> Kind Regards,
> Dan"

An email address soon followed, and I was then able to get to work on crafting an effective sales email that contained some more information but was designed to continue the conversation and, ideally, move it onto a phone call or face-to-face meeting.

The email described our packages in more detail, explained some of the other companies we had worked with and the results (ROI) that they had achieved. The email ended with: "If it's something that you're interested in, I would love to pop in and explore in a bit more detail."

A meeting was confirmed, where I learned all about the company, their past, present and plans for the future. It was clear they had a real need for what I was selling; however, I was also made aware they were exploring other companies as well.

We explored how this product could fit well, how it could work, and what the process would be following this meeting. They had to run it past the CEO before looking at a more detailed plan of action.

A couple of weeks later, I followed up with a phone call. The meeting had been delayed with the CEO, but they were pushing for it this week.

I then received a phone call later that week after the meeting had happened, informing me they were keen to move forward and wanted me to come in to work out a more detailed plan of implementation.

There were two more meetings and several emails back and forth while the final proposal was drawn up and then finally presented.

The process from start to finish took around five months. After finally presenting the proposal, I was met with the response I had worked so hard for:

Eighty units at £15,000 each across four years were ordered, a deal worth a total of £1,200,000.

One of the biggest sales of my entire sales career.

That whole deal, that whole million-pound deal, started with one single LinkedIn message.

Not a cold call, not a cold email, not a referral, not a networking event, but one simple single LinkedIn message.

It's not the phone VERSUS social selling.

One of the biggest debates that has raged across sales for several years now is the whole phone/cold calling versus social selling. It gets heated, emotional and often quite aggressive. Unfortunately, I've been involved in several debates over recent years, but my message has always been this:

> It's not the phone/cold calling VERSUS social selling; it's the phone/cold calling ALONGSIDE social selling.

As you'll see from my example of the million-pound LinkedIn message, it was social selling that created the opportunity and the phone that then progressed it, alongside email and face-to-face meetings.

It was the combination of all of these platforms that allowed me to sell effectively and win this deal. I guarantee there would have been other salespeople approaching this prospect but only using the phone or even only using social media.

As Tony J Hughes describes it perfectly in his book, *COMBO Prospecting*: It's only by using all of these tools together that you can strategically sell to the modern-day customer.

The £1,000,000 wasn't won JUST on socials but was won through a combination of all the key tools out there. It was, however, created on socials, and this is why I'm so passionate about Social Selling. Had I not utilised social selling, I may never have created or won this deal.

THE PROCESS

Here's a summary of that process:

Stage 1 - Find a decision-maker on LinkedIn

Stage 2 - Send personalised connection request

Stage 3 - Send prospective message

Stage 4 - Ask for email to send information

Stage 5 - Send email with information

Stage 6 - Follow up and arrange phone call to discuss

Stage 7 - Have phone call and follow up with email

Stage 8 - Arrange face-to-face meeting

Stage 9 - Have face-to-face meeting

Stage 10 - Send follow-up email

Stage 11 - Build proposal

Stage 12 - Present proposal

Stage 13 - Follow up to close deal

Stage 14 - Close deal and sign paperwork

Stage 15 - Implement product/service

Stage 16 - Gain referrals and a recommendation

And there you have it. . .

One simple LinkedIn message aimed at starting a prospecting conversation turned into an email with more information, which turned into a phone call to discuss in more detail, which turned into a face-to-face meeting to discuss a potential opportunity, which, after a few more emails and meetings, turned into a signed deal.

As I've already mentioned that message template won't work for everyone.

This is why I've included 25 templates in this book.

What I hope you'll see is that the £1,000,000 message and all of the other templates have a few things in common. . .

They're light, conversational and serve the same purpose of START-ING the conversation. In my experience, this is the best way to leverage LinkedIn to sell.

Right now, a percentage of decision-makers still prefer the phone as a communication method. However, younger decision-makers are rising, and current decision-makers are becoming more digital-savvy.

There are more and more people buying products, both B2C and B2B, through total digital conversation.

I currently have several key B2B clients where the whole conversation, from prospecting, to qualifying, presenting and closing, is done entirely on LinkedIn or other social media platforms.

Digital customers need digital sellers, so now is the best time to start learning and mastering the digital and social selling landscape. Learn to master all the aspects, including social media messaging.

Learn these message templates, find the prospects they are best suited for, personalise them and feel free to make changes. You should know your prospects better than anyone, so use these as guidance to help craft the ultimate message for your prospects.

CHAPTER 12

25 WRITTEN SALES MESSAGE TEMPLATES

There are so many ways you can craft effective LinkedIn messages, with the key always being to personalise them to each individual prospect and customer.

I'm going to share with you a set of templates that I have used over the years to generate sales opportunities selling IT, Software, Advertising, Training, Events and Consultancy.

NOTE: INSERT NAME – *You will notice that each template starts with this. It is because this is SO IMPORTANT!*

Personalisation is crucial when it comes to effective sales messaging. As I mention earlier in the book, messaging becomes significantly less effective when you adopt the "copy and paste" approach. It is worth the effort to ensure that you use your prospect's name to help deliver the optimal impact of the message.

THE GOAL OF THE MESSAGE

You will notice that most of these templates focus on the goal of opening the conversation or gaining an email address to send information across. When it comes to social selling and LinkedIn, this approach has become the most successful, in my experience, compared to outright asking for a phone call or face-to-face meeting. By offering to send more information with the aim of securing an email address, you open the doors to conversation. Going in for the kill and asking for a call or meeting is extremely "sales-y" and aggressive.

> *"But Dan, that's what we do when we cold call. We want to speak to them and get a meeting."*

True, but that's why ROI on cold calling is often below 2–3%. The phone and socials are different platforms; we use them both very differently.

I fully suggest you leverage cold calling and make your 50–100+ calls per day or whatever you need to make. However, when leveraging social selling and, more specifically, LinkedIn messaging, my advice is to use it to start conversations or get your foot in the door where you can then EARN the opportunity to arrange a phone call or meeting.

You'll notice the usage of SOFTER words as well. . .

Throughout these templates, you'll notice words like "believe," "possibly," "potentially," "maybe," etc. These are soft words and ones that aren't often encouraged in sales; however, when it comes to social selling and utilising messaging on LinkedIn, it's these words that I've found deliver the best results.

Instead of "Hi, my name's Dan, and I'm confident I could help you with my product," write "Hi, my name's Dan, and I believe we may be able to help you with this product."

You avoid coming across as ego-driven or arrogant and also avoid sounding like an aggressive salesperson. Instead, the message and tone are focused far more on helping them and how you believe you may be able to.

I've tried and tested stronger, more assertive language in LinkedIn messages, and I've tried and tested softer language, and, in my experience, the softer language delivers a far greater response rate.

Let's get into these templates. . .

After testing hundreds of templates over the last six years through my own prospecting, with my sales teams and with the businesses I have trained, here are the 25 that have proven to be the most effective:

1. THE INTRODUCTION MESSAGE

Hi (Insert Name),

Thank you for connecting. I work for a company called (Insert company name), who is one of the world's/region's/local areas' best in (insert product/service). If I can ever help you, please do let me know.

Kind Regards,
Dan

> NOTE: This works well as a friendly initial introduction. You're not asking for anything, just letting them know what it is you do and that you are there if they need it.

If you catch someone at the right time when they need what you sell, this message will generate a good response and is a great way to start the conversation because it's not aggressive or pushy, just a simple introduction.

Some salespeople use this template, but instead of ending it with "if I can ever help," they go straight in and ask for a phone call or meeting.

This can come across as pushy and given the high chance you've never met or spoken to this person, it doesn't give them much reason to speak to you. Instead, keep it open, let them know what you do, and then step away to focus on other social selling activities, such as personal brand and content.

I'd advise sending this message and then starting to work on engaging with their content. *"Like"* and comment on some of their posts, get your name before them and show interest, knowledge and value.

Take it a step further by regularly sharing your own content. This will build your personal brand and build their trust.

Then after a few weeks, pop them another message more focused on a potential ROI and ask to send them some more information (you'll see some examples of these messages below).

2. THE ROI INTRODUCTION

Hi (Insert Name),

I wanted to pop you a quick message to let you know that we help businesses (insert ROI) with (insert product).

If you ever need (insert product), please feel free to get in touch for an informal chat.

Kind Regards,
Dan

NOTE: A slight adjustment to the first template, this one is another introduction-style post but with the addition of ROI.

I've used this when approaching more senior decision-makers and C-Level prospects as the ROI cuts through the noise more effectively.

Showing them what you can do for them can act like a strong bait. I used this one with a recruitment company that brought me in; we crafted this message:

Hi (Insert Name),

I wanted to pop you a quick message to let you know that we help businesses save up to 80% of their recruitment costs with our "straight to job board" system.

If you would ever like to know a bit more, please do let me know.

Kind Regards,
Joe Bloggs

Again, this is a nice, soft introduction-style message but one that is attached with a potential ROI, which then becomes bait.

As a salesperson, by sending this message out to prospects, it's like casting fishing rods out into the river or sea. If there are fish (prospects) who are ready to bite, they'll bite and reply, and you can then reel them in.

If they are not ready, that message will sit out there until they are (whilst you utilise other social selling methods). The beauty of this message is that for some, your name will stick in their head, and they'll remember what it is that you do.

3. THE PROBLEM SOLVER

Hi (Insert Name),

Thank you for connecting.

I'd love to see if we may be able to help you (insert problem solved) with (insert product/service)?

Kind Regards,
Dan

NOTE: This one is a step up from the introduction-style post and goes in with a soft question, essentially asking to talk. You thank them for connecting and then tell them how you would love to help them solve a particular problem with the product or service that you sell.

You ask in the form of a question so that those who have that problem and would like it solved are more inclined to then reply and open the conversation.

This is a light message, quite soft and very simple. It's not packed with tonnes of features and benefits or a massive sales pitch, just a simple comment that you may be able to help them achieve something.

4. THE VIDEO MESSAGE

Hi (Insert Name),

If you can spare three minutes, here is a quick video of how we're helping similar companies to yours achieve (insert ROI) with (insert product) – (insert YouTube link or video).

Kind Regards,
Dan

NOTE: A video is already an amazing sales tool and communication method, and LinkedIn gives you the opportunity to send videos through messages.

There are two ways you can do this: You can copy the link to a YouTube video or other hosted video, or you can attach it directly. These videos should be 2–3 minutes long max and fully personalised.

Make sure you're passionate about it; you need to be comfortable in front of the camera, so lots of practice first is highly recommended.

If you can, I'd also recommend using subtitles/captions as well. A lot of people are using LinkedIn in a working office and so often can't actually listen to any content online. Having subtitles means they can still consume the video in their working day.

I use a platform called Zubtitle (other great ones are available as well). It's reasonably priced and super-easy to use. You upload the video, it adds the captions, you check them to make sure they're right, and then you download it.

The big advantage of video is it's the closest thing to face-to-face interaction, which is the ultimate form of interaction you can have with a prospect.

They can see you, look into your eyes and see the confidence and passion that you have for your product and industry and in helping them.

5. LOOKING FOR LEADERSHIP INSIGHT

Hi (Insert Name),

I'm looking for some information from (insert industry) leaders around how they do (insert subject). Would you be able to contribute?

Kind Regards,
Dan

> NOTE: A great way to get your foot in the door with a potential client is to ask for their thoughts, knowledge and experience.

This works very well for tough decision-makers, people who perhaps have quite small networks or who have large networks but are active on socials. Sometimes this shows a large ego, and so asking for them to contribute feeds into that.

Not only will you gather great information that will help you, but you'll also build a stronger foundation for the relationship compared to going straight in for the sale.

You can angle this around a specific blog that you're looking to write or even an industry whitepaper that your company is putting together. It feels great to be needed and to have your insights wanted for something relevant to the industry.

I've done this many times over the years, and it's helped carve some strong relationships and generate some very strong opportunities.

6. THE CASE STUDY INTRODUCTION

Hi (Insert name),

Last month, we worked with (insert customer company). They spent X and achieved an ROI of (insert ROI). I've had a look through your profile, and I believe we may be able to help you achieve something similar. Would it be possible to send you a little bit of information?

Kind Regards,
Dan

NOTE: Another template very powerful with higher-level decision-makers, this one lays out not just an ROI but evidence of how a company similar to theirs, and hopefully a company they will know or recognise, has achieved it.

It's important that this is 100% proven and factual and that you have a full case study or testimonial to send them if they ask.

This works by sparking interest in either the company that you mention or the ROI that they have achieved. This is a lot different from most of the messages that prospects will receive, which are usually more focused on the salesperson and not the prospect.

This one is built for them—it's showing them that you have something that could and hopefully would benefit them, and you've got proof of how it has helped someone similar.

If you've got the case study available as a nice document, you could even attach that to the message as well so they can open it and read the full thing, giving them more confidence in you and growing their interest in what you're offering.

7. THE FREE TRIAL OR DEMO OFFER

Hi (Insert Name),

Are you looking to save money (or another ROI) on your (insert product)?

If so, I would love to help and offer you a free trial/demo of (insert product).

Kind Regards,
Dan

NOTE: Many salespeople out there will offer a free trial or demo of their product to help get into a company, show them their product and increase their chances of then closing the deal.

This message is built to show them the potential ROI that they could achieve and then offer them the opportunity to try before they buy!

You're ultimately trying to create a "what have you got to lose" situation. Once they see that and hopefully agree, the free trial or demo then opens the door to the conversation and creates a sales opportunity for you.

If they don't reply, utilise other platforms such as the phone, email and post to ensure your message gets in front of them.

8. THE EVENT INVITATION

Hi (Insert Name),

I'm running an event at (insert location) on (insert date) and thought it might be something that would interest you. Would you like a free ticket to attend?

Kind Regards,
Dan

NOTE: Inviting someone to an event is a great way to prospect and create opportunities and inviting them via LinkedIn can be a powerful way to do it.

As we all know, most decision-makers receive hundreds of emails every day, so when you send them an invite via email, there is a high chance it will get ignored or sent to the spam folder.

Sending a nice, short message like this often stands a higher chance of being seen and responded to. You can add a small amount of extra detail, perhaps mentioning what is going to be covered. For example, "We will have a Microsoft Expert in to discuss the latest technologies on the horizon."

If they reply, it's a win-win situation. If they say yes, it's a win—you get them to your event and have the opportunity to impress them and create a future opportunity.

If they say no, it's still a win as they're now talking to you—you've opened the lines of communication. They'll give you a reason, which will open up a warmer conversation.

If they just say no, a good way to try and keep the opportunity alive is to offer some form of industry research document, guide or eBook.

You're still offering something of value, knowledge and insight but without the need for them to move past their computer. There is a decent chance they'll accept, and again, this creates the opportunity to talk.

You can follow up with a message after a few days, asking if they have had a chance to read it or give them a call to discuss it.

9. WOULD YOU LIKE AN EBOOK?

Hi (Insert Name),

We've just released a new eBook on the latest (insert industry) trends. Would you like a copy?

Kind Regards,
Dan

NOTE: Following on from the previous template and the opportunity to send them an eBook, this message template offers that straight away. Perhaps you can't put on an event, or you'd like quicker results.

Offering them a strong piece of industry content is a nice way to give something first and create a warm conversation starter.

If they say yes, then send it and, similar to the message template above, follow up to discuss it a few days after. If they say no, perhaps look at sending the email directly with the content attached or, even better, print it off and send it via post.

Decision-makers will rarely receive something like that printed, so it could make a good impact. Even if they say yes on LinkedIn, you could send them a digital copy and send a printed one as well for extra bonus points!

An eBook or guide only needs to be ten pages long, ideally visually strong, and containing some valuable insight or knowledge.

If you have a marketing department, they should be able to create one quite easily. If you don't have a marketing department, you'll be able to find plenty of free templates via Google or use Microsoft PowerPoint to create one and save it as a PDF copy to send.

10. LINKEDIN RECOMMENDED YOU

Hi (Insert Name),

You came up as a suggestion on LinkedIn today as someone I should connect with. I've had a look at your profile and think we may be able to help. We provide (insert product/service) to help companies like yours achieve (insert ROI).

Would it be ok to send you some more information?

Kind Regards,
Dan

NOTE: If you go into the "My Network" section on your LinkedIn profile, LinkedIn will give you a list of suggestions of people you could or should connect with. Within these lists are often prospects or people who work within prospective companies.

This is an effective template to use because it informs them that it was LinkedIn who recommended they connect, and as the platform that you're on, it's pretty trustworthy!

You then go on to find and give them the reason why the connection made sense and how you think you could help them.

> TOP TIP: Alongside effective LinkedIn messaging, I would highly recommend that you grow your network on a daily basis.
>
> Using LinkedIn suggestions is a great place to start, and I recommend adding at least ten people each day. I wouldn't add more than 25–35 per day because you'll increase the chance that LinkedIn will block your account for over-adding.

If they don't reply, this will warm up the cold call a bit as you can reference the fact that LinkedIn recommended them to you and that after doing some research, you believe that you may be able to help them.

11. CARDS ON THE TABLE

Hi (Insert Name),

We have a (new) product (insert product) that does (insert solution). I'm confident we could help you achieve (insert potential ROI) with it. Would it be possible to send you some more information?

Kind Regards,
Dan

NOTE: Being honest and upfront can be a powerful tool in sales. It's important to remember your prospects are receiving tonnes of spammy sales messages on LinkedIn, via email and through cold calls every single day.

Very few will be upfront and honest that they're trying to sell something, and so when a salesperson does put their cards on the table, it can have a strong impact.

This message lays it all out simply, showing them what you offer and what it can help them achieve.

12. THE SHARED LINKEDIN GROUP

Hi (Insert Name),

We're both part of the (insert group name) group. I've actually been working with a few companies very similar to yours, helping them with (insert problem solved or ROI). Would it be possible to send you some information on how we may be able to do the same for you?

Kind Regards,
Dan

NOTE: I'll be honest—groups on LinkedIn right now are not great. I live in the hope that LinkedIn will breathe new life into them, taking some advice from Facebook where groups thrive.

However, I would never advise you to ignore them altogether. There are still tonnes of groups out there, some with thousands, tens of thousands, or even hundreds of thousands of members.

It can be quite valuable to join industry groups and use the group as an introduction topic through messaging. Stating that you are in the same group as them will make you appear a lot warmer than just a cold salesperson.

You could reference a recent piece of content shared in the group or look for some engagement and interaction that they've done and reference that.

BONUS TIP: Why not create your own industry group?! Build one that is totally neutral, so not associated with your company, and invite many of your prospects into it.

You can then control the content and use the group as a conversation starter with your prospects. Invite industry experts to contribute and build something that becomes a real value to everyone who is involved.

13. MUTUAL CONNECTION OR REFERRAL

Hi (Insert Name),

(Insert mutual connection/referral) suggested that I pop you a quick message as you may be able to benefit from what we offer here.

We help people with our (insert product) to solve (insert problem). Would it be ok to send you a bit of information about what we do?

Kind Regards,
Dan

NOTE: Firstly, it is VERY important that if you are using this template, you are 100% positive that your prospect knows the person you're going to reference! I say this for one simple reason: Just because someone is connected to someone on LinkedIn, it doesn't mean that they actually know them.

If I contact a prospect and say, "John Smith suggested I pop you a message," and it turns out that my prospect has no idea who John Smith is, it backfires quickly! LinkedIn might even be telling me that John Smith is a mutual connection; however, it doesn't mean that they actually know them.

This works well when you have a referral or have actually been recommended by a mutual connection to reach out.

If you're unsure, ask your mutual connection. Back to the example above, I could message John Smith and ask him whether he actually knows my prospect.

I could ask him to introduce me, or even if he's not willing to do that, if I can confirm that he knows him, then I can use the above template.

14. THE HONESTY MESSAGE

Hi (Insert name),

I'd love the opportunity to try to sell to you (insert product). I'm being completely honest here because I'm pretty confident that it's something that will help you. If afterwards you believe it's not right for you, then I'll happily leave you alone.

Would it be possible to send you some information or give you a call later this week?

Kind Regards,
Dan

NOTE: This is similar to the cards on the table message but taken a step further where you lay out from the start that you're trying to sell them something.

This same approach works well on cold calls, where you open the call by admitting it is a cold call, and then you ask for 30 seconds to tell them what it is about, and if they're not interested, you can leave it at that.

What you're doing is showing honesty from the start, but you're telling them you believe you can help them achieve something. Because you've opened with honesty, they're suddenly more likely to believe you when you tell them that you think you can help them.

It's one of the rare scenarios in sales where being honest that you're a salesperson actually helps BUILD trust!

15. DID YOU GET MY LETTER. . .?

Hi (Insert Name),

I just wanted to see if you got my letter in the post?

Kind Regards,
Dan

> NOTE: Obviously, this template requires you to send a letter, but it creates another great opportunity to prospect. Few salespeople send letters anymore, so doing that in itself can be a powerful prospecting tool. Then following it up by messaging everyone you've sent letters to on LinkedIn can help increase conversions.

Let's say you sent 100 letters, and ten got back to you. By contacting the other 90 via LinkedIn, you could convert another 10+ prospects. It's important to keep the LinkedIn message super-short and simple, as this increases the chance you'll get a reply. It will encourage them to either acknowledge it, check to find the letter or tell you no, in which case, you can confirm the details and send it again.

16. YOU'RE USING OUR COMPETITOR

Hi (Insert Name),

I noticed on your website/our competitors' website that you're currently using (insert competitor).

We offer a very similar product but which has more features and at a more competitive price. Would it be ok to send you some information to see if you'd like to explore?

Kind Regards,
Dan

NOTE: This is one of my favourite templates and one I've used many, many times. What I like most about this is that you're upfront and honest that they're using your competitor but that you think you could offer them a better deal.

A lot of decision-makers, whilst sometimes on the front of it are loyal to their suppliers, are always keen to know what other options are out there.

They have numbers to hit as well, pressures and targets on them, and if you can get them closer to that than the company they're currently using, they're usually open to looking into it.

It's honest but not in an aggressive or confrontational way, just simply stating that they clearly need what you sell, and your product might offer them more.

17. THE ROI QUESTION

Hi (Insert Name),

If I could save you (insert ROI) on your (insert problem), would you be interested?

Kind Regards,
Dan

NOTE: Whilst the same in some ways as previous templates, this one is a little more to the point. You're asking them straight out if you could achieve something for them, would they be interested.

For example, going back to the previous example (Template #2) about the recruitment firm pitching to save up to 80% of recruitment costs, they may write something like this:

Hi John,

If I could save you 80% on your recruitment costs, would you be interested?

Kind Regards,
Dan

Imagine sending that to a hiring manager or business owner, who would be spending thousands, if not tens of thousands, a year on recruitment costs. It's an attractive bait that will often generate a strong number of bites, with people replying, "Yes, I would be interested."

This then opens the door for you to send information and start that all-important conversation.

18. RECENT ACTIVITY OBSERVATION

Hi (Insert Name),

I noticed today/yesterday/recently that you wrote about (insert recent post subject). This is something I've seen time and again, and you high-light it perfectly; it was a really great post! What do you think (insert subject-relevant question)?

Kind Regards,
Dan

> NOTE: When you visit your prospects' LinkedIn profiles, search their recent activity and look for a piece of content that you can leverage to start a conversation.

That could be a post that they had written, a video they recorded, it could be a post following an industry event they went to or even a blog they shared or wrote.

The key is to compliment them on the post and then ask a question about the subject. Equally, if there is something you disagree with, feel free to challenge them on it (politely or professionally!). The aim is to encourage a response that can then open the door to conversation.

It's a good opportunity for you to showcase your interest and knowledge of the industry and to start a neutral conversation based on a shared interest, not just you wanting to sell them something!

Messages like this template follow the theme of not trying to jump in bed with your prospect straight away.

19. THE PROFILE VIEW

Hi (Insert Name),

I noticed today you viewed my profile OR Thank you for viewing my profile today. I'd love to know what your company is currently doing/ using for (insert product/solution)?

Kind Regards,
Dan

NOTE: This is another one of my favourite templates and one that has generated a lot of revenue for me over the years. It's also one of the most under-used areas of social selling.

Every day, people are viewing your profile (they should if you're active on LinkedIn). A percentage of those people will be prospects, and it's a tremendous opportunity for you to see when they've looked at your profile.

I'll share a case study I use in my training sessions that certainly brings this template to life:

After checking my profile views, which I do once or twice a day, I noticed that the Managing Director and Sales Director of the same company had viewed my profile. Now, I sell three things personally, LinkedIn training, Keynote Speaking and Advertising for *The Daily Sales*. I could quickly see that this would be a potential interest in LinkedIn/Social Selling.

It had been three hours since they had both viewed my profile, and I hadn't received a LinkedIn message or an email from either of them.

What had happened, which I later found out, was that they were having their regular weekly meeting, and the topic of social selling came up. Both were connected with me on LinkedIn and had seen my content and activity. They discussed potential training and then moved on to the many other things to discuss about the business. Now, clearly for them at that time, it wasn't a pressing need for them to reach out to me; perhaps they would have done later that day, later that week, maybe even later that month.

We all know what it's like—we discuss tonnes of these things daily, but they often sit on the back burner. After noticing that they had viewed my profile and qualifying them as a potential prospect, I sent them both the Profile View LinkedIn message following this exact template.

I had a reply within ten minutes from the Managing Director. It read:

"Thanks for your message, Dan. Yes, we were discussing this today. We currently use LinkedIn a bit, but we would be interested to see if there is more we could do with it. Could you speak to my Sales Director to explore?"

He helped me arrange a phone call, which led to three phone calls, two face-to-face meetings and one lunch before they hired me to train their company. Now they may have reached out to me, but as a true hunter and sales professional, I didn't want to leave something like this to chance.

Ensure you check your profile views regularly, qualify those who could be prospects, and use that profile view as the opportunity to start a conversation.

20. THE DIRECT PROFILE VIEW MESSAGE

Hi (Insert Name),

I noticed you viewed my profile today. Are you possibly looking at (insert product/solution)?

Kind Regards,
Dan

> NOTE: A more direct version of the profile view message. Instead of asking loosely what they're doing relevant to your product/industry, this one goes straight to the question of whether they are looking specifically for what it is you sell.

I'd recommend only using this one once you've qualified that they could be a potential prospect. I tend to use this one after a few days of the profile view (changing the today part) and use it as a follow-up message for those who haven't replied.

21. THE ENGAGEMENT THANK-YOU

Hi (Insert Name),

Thank you for liking my recent blog/post/video on LinkedIn! What were your thoughts on (insert content topic)?

Kind Regards,
Dan

NOTE: In a similar context to your profile views, the engagement on the content you share and create is another fantastic door-opening opportunity. Once again, let me bring this particular template to life with a case study:

When I was selling in the IT sector, I had not long started writing my own sales blog on LinkedIn as well. I'd publish an article a week on sales via LinkedIn, and they would gain some average engagement each time. Obviously, whilst sharing these blogs, I was looking to reach IT Managers and IT Directors of small- to medium-sized companies.

One company in particular that I was prospecting was proving extremely tough to get through to. I'd tried cold calling multiple times, left voicemails, and sent emails; I just couldn't get the attention of the decision-maker (something I'm sure a lot of salespeople will relate to).

After sharing another one of my sales blogs one week, I noticed that one of the sales reps at that company had clicked 'like' on my article. I realised that whilst not the decision-maker themselves, they could hold the key to the decision-maker. I sent them a LinkedIn message following the Engagement template. The salesperson replied straight away, and over a few messages, we discussed the topic of the blog.

After building some rapport, I earned the opportunity to mention what I was selling. *"Actually, I wonder if you could help me? I've been trying to speak to your IT Manager about what we sell but am struggling to get through to them!"*

The salesperson was more than happy to help, providing me with an internal introduction and arranging a phone call. I then used that phone call to book a face-to-face meeting and turned that into a confirmed sale.

Now a big part of utilising this particular message template is the requirement that you share or create content that drives engagement. Unfortunately, there is so much to this that I physically can't fit it all into this book! If you're interested in learning how to create the best possible content on LinkedIn, have a look at www.danieldisney .online.

22. GOING TO THE SAME EVENT

Hi (Insert Name),

I noticed that you are going to (insert event) next week. I'm going to be there as well and would love the opportunity to buy you a coffee. Do you have any free time in the morning or afternoon?

Kind Regards,
Dan

OR

Hi (Insert Name),

Next week is the (insert industry event), and I wondered if you were planning to attend?

Kind Regards,
Dan

NOTE: Attending key events is a core part of networking and prospecting for many salespeople. Messaging prospects beforehand can be a unique way to book in meetings at the event before it happens, helping increase your chances of success.

There are two ways to utilise this message. The first is if you know that they are attending. Perhaps their company posted that they were attending, or perhaps they posted about it on their feed.

Either way, if you know they're attending, you have an opportunity to invite them for a coffee or lunch to chat with you whilst you're there.

The other way is assuming you don't know whether or not they're attending an event. You can use this opportunity to message them and ask if they are planning to attend.

If they are, you'll know and then be able to ask if they'd like to grab a coffee. If they aren't attending, you've brought the event to their attention, showing that you are immersed in your industry.

23. THE SHARING CONTENT MESSAGE

Hi (Insert Name),

I've just published an article/post/video on LinkedIn on your industry (insert industry). I'd love to know your thoughts!

Kind Regards
Dan

> NOTE: Another sound way to start a conversation is to give value by sharing a piece of content that you think they will enjoy or benefit from.

I must stress, you need to make sure the first time you use this on a prospect that the content you choose to share with them is as good as possible. If you send them something that isn't good, you'll decrease the chance they'll read anything else from you.

Find or create an amazing piece of content that is absolutely packed with value for them and send it. You can expand this message a bit to describe what's included in the content or why you think it would be valuable to them.

The aim is to get them to read/watch/listen to the content so that you can then use it to create a conversation. With the right content, you are also able to make a good first impression with them and potentially build the layers of trust as well.

24. THE RESEARCH MESSAGE

Hi (Insert Name),

I don't want to waste your time, but I've done some research on you and (insert their company) and believe we could help you achieve (insert ROI).

Could I send you a quick email, and if it's something you're potentially interested in, perhaps we could jump on a call?

Kind Regards,
Dan

> NOTE: The reason this template works so well is that you are showing effort; you are showing them that you have done the research and believe you can help. A lot of salespeople, especially in years past, would just phone cold data from a spreadsheet.

They had no idea who they were phoning or whether that person would benefit. What this template does is the opposite; it shows them that you HAVE researched them and believe you can actually help them.

I must stress that this isn't one that can be copied, pasted and sent to everyone in your network. You actually do have to research them, qualify them and have a good reason for wanting to message them.

It's worth that extra effort, though, trust me. This is how you stop wasting time trying to sell to anyone and everyone and start investing your time talking to the right people whom you are more likely to actually convert into sales.

25. THE MISSED CALL MESSAGE

Hi (Insert Name),

I tried to call you today, but you were busy. I noticed on your profile that you are the (insert job title) at (insert company). I believe we may be able to help you achieve (insert ROI) and wondered if I could send you some more information by email?

Kind Regards,
Dan

> NOTE: The power of this one is that it shows you made an effort and tried to phone them. For a lot of people, this is the sign of a strong salesperson and not just someone sending spammy messages one after the other. I must say that it is very important that you ACTUALLY do try to call them!

I can imagine some salespeople trying to "hack" their way with this, sending loads of LinkedIn messages saying they tried to call, and then when the prospect checks and finds out they didn't actually call, creating a bigger problem!

However, for a lot of you reading this book, you will already be making tonnes of cold calls each day and following up each of those on LinkedIn with a message like this can really help.

CHAPTER 13

TOP WRITTEN MESSAGE TIPS

As I mentioned at the start, sending written messages on LinkedIn is still, and always will be, an incredibly effective form of prospecting and communication. Some people out there prefer a written message over any other form.

Hopefully this chapter and the templates in Chapter 12 gave you everything you need to begin sending more effective written messages. In addition, I would like to add some of my top tips:

- You should only send messages to people whom you genuinely believe you can help. Before messaging, pre-qualify them first.

- You should also do some level of research on the person before you send a message to give you an opportunity to personalise it.
- Remember, the more you make the message about them, the more likely it will be that you'll get a reply.
- Sending messages outside of common working hours can be an effective strategy as a lot of decision-makers are busy between 9 and 5.
- Sending messages at the weekend is also something to consider with a lot of people just as active and potentially more available.
- Keep them short and sweet; they are an instant message, not an email.
- Before you click send, read it and put yourself in their shoes. Would you read and reply to that message?
- If they don't reply to your written message, avoid sending another written message to follow up. Instead, look to try an audio or video message (as covered in the upcoming chapters).

PART 5
AUDIO LINKEDIN MESSAGES

CHAPTER 14

AUDIO VOICE NOTES ON LINKEDIN

Imagine being one of the first salespeople to make cold calls, back when the phone was a novelty, back when getting a call on your phone was one of the most exciting things to happen. Many today might find it hard to believe, but there was a time when it would make your day to get a call on your phone and talking on it was just as exciting.

Back then, I can imagine the conversion rates on sales calls were incredibly high because there wouldn't have been many salespeople phoning people, so the ones that did would often clean up.

Now imagine being one of the first salespeople to send a prospecting email. Back when people didn't get many emails, each one would be opened and read with interest. Fast forward to now, it's safe to say the majority of people hate getting cold-called, hate getting calls from unknown phone numbers, and rarely answer them. (No, I'm not suggesting cold calling is dead; whilst I said *many*, there are still people who do answer calls!) As for email, people get hundreds each day, with their email addresses programmed into multiple cadence and marketing tools (again, I'm not saying that email doesn't work, it does, it's just a lot more challenging than it used to be).

Well, whilst it's nice taking a trip down memory lane, what if that opportunity existed today to use something that was new, something that not many salespeople were using, and something people got excited to receive?

Sounds exciting, right?

Well, it's very much true, and it very much exists, so let me show you.

I recently ran a poll on *The Daily Sales* LinkedIn page, on which 7,248 salespeople voted.

The results of that poll didn't surprise me, but they may surprise you. What the results do show is one of the BIGGEST opportunities for salespeople right now. . .

If 94% of salespeople aren't doing this yet, now is your time to get ahead.

The poll that I shared asked one simple question. . .

How many audio voice messages do you send on LinkedIn per day?

(I'm going to show you exactly how to send them in this article, so keep reading if you want to create more sales opportunities and pipelines with them.)

Before we continue, let me highlight some of the REPLIES & RESPONSES that I have received and have seen from other salespeople who have been sending audio voice messages on LinkedIn from their prospects:

"I didn't know you could send messages like this on LinkedIn! Thank you, I'd love some more information."

"This message was great! Yes, I'm interested in booking a meeting."

"No one has sent me an audio message before, good job! I'm open to hearing more about your product."

Let me explain why this is such an exciting opportunity, just like COLD CALLING used to be. . .

Can you imagine being one of the first salespeople ever to make cold calls? Back all those years ago when the phone was still new, and people LOVED getting phone calls?! The salespeople who were brave and bold enough to make them cleaned up.

Well, audio voice notes are still new, especially to LinkedIn and especially in the B2B space.

Even out of the 6% of salespeople that are sending them, 4% are sending only 1–10 per day.

To help, I'm going to show you EXACTLY how to send them and what to say. Read on for more in Chapter 15.

CHAPTER 15

HOW TO SEND AUDIO VOICE NOTES ON LINKEDIN

Using the mobile LinkedIn app, when you log in and go to send a message, you will see a microphone icon next to the space where you would normally write the message.

When you select that button, you'll see the above pop-up. When you're ready, you'll need to press AND hold that blue section in the middle with the microphone on it. You need to keep it held for as long as you're recording, and when you're finished, take your finger off the button.

NOTE: You can record up to a maximum of 60 seconds per audio voice note.

Once you've finished, the app prompts you and asks if you want to send the message. If you made any mistakes (we all do, it's normal!), you can cancel it and record it again until you get it right. When you're happy, click send, and the message will send.

BIG QUICK SALES TIP: Audio voice notes are the perfect follow-up message.

If you've sent a written message to a prospect (and you can go back 6–12 months) and they HAVEN'T replied to you, go back and try sending an audio voice note instead.

What are my top tips when sending audio voice messages on LinkedIn?

1) Practice, practice, practice. If you're nervous or have never recorded one before, just start recording some voice memos on your phone to get comfortable with doing it. It will make you feel more confident and will help you get used to doing it.

2) Focus on your TONE. Stand up if you can, smile when you speak and make sure you're engaging.

3) Keep them short, sweet and to the point. Even though they're only 60 seconds, if you want them to listen all the way through and reply, you need to give them a good reason to do so.

4) Avoid sending more than one if it's the first message you're sending. If the audio message is your first or prospecting message, only send one; try not to send multiple so that you can send more than 60 seconds' worth.

5) Make sure the audio message is about THEM, what you think you can do for them, how they will benefit, etc. It's not about what you're trying to sell but how it will help them.

So, if you want to get ahead of your competition, start sending more audio voice messages!

Successful audio voice notes generate responses just like this:

"Wow, I didn't know you could even do this on LinkedIn! Yes, I'd love to learn more about that."

"You're the first person to ever send me an audio message on here. Thank you! Please send me more information to. . ."

"It's great to get a message from a real person and not something automated. I'm not the right person to speak to, but here are the details for who you should approach. . ."

I'm hoping that if you are one of the 94% of people not sending voice notes, you're now starting to see the opportunity in front of you. This is why I knew writing *The Ultimate LinkedIn Messaging Guide* was crucial and why, in the following chapters, I show you how and when to do it, and I'll provide multiple scripts you can use.

WHEN TO SEND AUDIO VOICE NOTES

Audio voice notes can be used at any time, and there is little evidence that they are more effective at different stages of the sales process. At the beginning of this book, we discussed the prospecting maze, showing how different people prefer to communicate in different ways. It's the same on LinkedIn; some people love audio voice notes, and others hate them. There are people who love video messages and people who hate them, and there are people who love written messages whilst others do not.

PROSPECTING – Audio voice notes can be incredibly effective as a first-touch prospecting message.

FOLLOW-UP – If you've made a cold call and left a voicemail, sent an email, or even sent a previous LinkedIn message, an audio voice note is great for following up.

CLOSING – After you've sent over the contract, an audio voice note can make a great message to confirm what the next-step options are.

ACCOUNT MANAGEMENT – Don't wait for formal chats with your accounts. Send voice notes on a semi-frequent basis so they feel valued.

CHAPTER 16

THE TWO MOST IMPORTANT COMPONENTS

Whilst there are many things to consider when sending an audio voice note, such as research, personalisation, timing, etc., there are two components above all that are the most important.

Those are:

- TONE
- RELEVANCE

When people listen to an audio voice note, your tone impacts what they think of you and your message, and the relevance will determine whether they act as a result of your message.

TONE

If you're a cold caller and have had good cold calling training, you should be a master at tone! Nothing I say here is new or different apart from treating an audio voice note tone the same way you would a cold call or a voicemail.

When changing or choosing the tone of your voice, consider these key areas:

- Inflection: Changing the pitch of your voice can make your words more exciting, energetic, or sincere.
- Emphasis: Underlining certain words can help convey enthusiasm and importance.
- Pace: Speaking too quickly can make you sound nervous or stressed; speaking too slowly can make you sound disinterested or unprofessional.

The biggest tip I'll give is to either stand up when recording voice notes or sit up with your back straight to ensure your voice sounds clear. When you're facing the table or floor or reading a script, it can negatively impact your tone and how your message is received.

Personally, I like to walk around when I record audio voice notes, which is exactly what I used to do when I was a cold caller back in the day.

RELEVANCE

We've already covered this in the book, so I'm not going to repeat it, but I do want to highlight that this is an incredibly important component that will directly determine whether or not your audio voice message gets a reply.

This is why I've included multiple templates to give you plenty of options to make your message relevant to each individual prospect.

CHAPTER 17

LINKEDIN AUDIO VOICE NOTE SALES SCRIPTS

Here are ten different scripts for audio voice note prospecting and sales messages that you can use. Remember, these are templates, they are simply the guide—you'll need to edit them to make them relevant to each prospect that you send them to.

With audio messages, you can record up to 60 seconds per message, and my advice is that for initial prospecting messages, you only send one single 60-second message. During conversations, you can then send multiple audio voice notes if what you need to say takes more than 60 seconds.

DISCLAIMER: Any names of people, companies and products are all fictional but merely used to give you the most real template possible for you to base yours upon.

AUDIO MESSAGE SCRIPT 1 – THE PLANTED SEED

"Hi Tom, I just wanted to say thank you for connecting. If you're ever looking to provide LinkedIn or Sales Navigator training for your sales team, please do let me know. I deliver live online programmes and in-person ones as well. If you'd ever like a little more information, just let me know, and I'll send some over."

NOTE: The goal of this audio message is simple, let them know what you do and where you are if they need you. If it's the right place/right time, then you might get an interested reply. But for everyone else, simply back this up by building your personal brand and sharing content on LinkedIn so that when they are ready, you're the person they go to.

AUDIO MESSAGE SCRIPT 2 – THE PROFILE RESEARCH

"Hi Holly, I had a little look through your profile and noticed that you're the SDR manager at Thrive, and it looks like you have around six SDRs in your team right now. I actually run a Social Selling Bootcamp for SDRs, which can help them book significantly

LINKEDIN AUDIO VOICE NOTE SALES SCRIPTS

more meetings through LinkedIn. If you like, I can send you a bit of information on what is covered."

> NOTE: You can't just pull random information from their LinkedIn profile, you need to make sure it's relevant to you, your product and/or your company.

AUDIO MESSAGE SCRIPT 3 – THE REFERRAL

"Hi John, last week, I delivered a two-day LinkedIn Masterclass with someone I believe you know, Sarah Smith, over at Pipedrive. Sarah said she would pop you a quick note as well, but she thought your team at Seamless might also greatly benefit from the training. If you would like, I'd be happy to jump on a quick call and talk you through what we covered in the training and see if it's the right fit for the team."

> NOTE: This has to be 100% verified and an official referral, which you will need to seek if you haven't already got one that you can use. Referrals are super-powerful as a lead generator and as a prospecting message.

AUDIO MESSAGE SCRIPT 4 – THE CONTENT REFERENCE

"Dale, I loved your post yesterday promoting your new team members—the team is growing so fast! Funnily enough, I actually worked with John a few years ago. He was fantastic, so you've got a good one there. Next time you're hiring, let me know, and I'll share

the job with my network. Might be a few other good connections that could be a good fit."

NOTE: This is a pure conversation-starting script, the goal simply being to build rapport and talk. If you wanted to turn this into a pitch message, you would simply change the "next time you're hiring" to:

"I'm imagining you've got a strong induction and training plan for those SDRs, but one thing I've noticed many companies struggling with is training their new SDRs on LinkedIn & Social Selling. I actually run an SDR bootcamp and can send you some more information on what we cover if you like."

AUDIO MESSAGE SCRIPT 5 – THE REAL ROI EXAMPLE

"Hey Thomas, we recently ran a sponsored webinar with Outreach where we generated 1,426 leads for them. I wanted to ask whether you think Clair might be interested in doing something similar? We completely run the webinar ourselves and include promoting the sponsor during advertisements, throughout the webinar itself and in the follow-up email with a recording. Our sponsors get all the registrant details, including full name, email, phone, company, location and role. If it's something you might be interested in, I'd love to talk you through some of the details."

NOTE: For this to work, these need to be real numbers that you can verify and prove if required.

AUDIO MESSAGE SCRIPT 6 – THE EVENT INVITE

"Hi Sam, are you attending the Marketing Leadership Summit this year? If you're not, I've got a free ticket and space at our table if you'd like to join us. Looks like a great line-up of speakers and sessions. We're inviting a few people from our LinkedIn networks, and I thought you might be interested in attending. If you are, let me know, and I'll send over the ticket and details."

NOTE: If you want to find events, type your target decision maker or prospect into the LinkedIn search bar and filter by events. This will bring up events coming up in your industry that your prospects might be attending or interested in. It's also worth doing an internet search for local or industry events that also might be relevant to them.

AUDIO MESSAGE SCRIPT 7 – THE FREE OFFER

"Hi Lilah, I was having a look through some of the LinkedIn profiles of your sales team, in particular John, Sarah, Clive and Harry, and I noticed quite a few gaps. I've done a quick assessment and wondered if you'd like me to send it over? It's completely free, but if you go through and see that there is an opportunity for training, I'd love to talk you through some of the LinkedIn & Social Selling programmes that we offer."

NOTE: Try to find something you can offer that will be valuable and relevant to them. It could be an eBook, webinar, training video, audit, insights, etc.

AUDIO MESSAGE SCRIPT 8 – THE COLD CALL

"Hi Frank, I tried to call you today and left a voicemail but thought I'd send you a quick voice note on LinkedIn as well. We've recently done some training with a few of your competitors, including Salesforce, HubSpot and Pipedrive, and I wanted to ask if the Dynamics sales team might benefit from some advanced social selling training? It covers all core areas, including messaging, content and personal branding, and can help salespeople increase their pipelines by up to 55%. If you're potentially interested, I could send you some more details via email."

NOTE: The perfect follow-up to an unanswered cold call is an audio voice message on LinkedIn!

AUDIO MESSAGE SCRIPT 9 – THE EXPERT ARTICLE

"Hi Brandon, my name is Dan, and I'm currently writing an article sharing the top-ten tips from sales experts, and I wondered if you would share one or two of your biggest tips for it? I'd love to include you in the article, which will link through to your LinkedIn profile and company page. If you're interested, let me know, and I'll send over some more details about the article and what we're looking for. I hope we can include you as part of it!"

NOTE: You'll see this template in all forms of messages in this book because it is an incredibly effective one that brings so much value. The key is that you actually write the article as well (which is in your best interest).

AUDIO MESSAGE SCRIPT 10 – THE THOUGHTFUL GIFT

"Hi Wendy, I had a quick look through your LinkedIn profile today and noticed you follow Jeb Blount, and I wondered if you'd been able to get a copy of his latest book? I actually have an extra copy and would love to send it to you if you'd like it. It focuses on selling in a crisis, which I know is going to help a lot of sales teams and I'm sure will be valuable for you and your team."

NOTE: Gifting is a powerful form of prospecting, and platforms like Reachdesk and Sendoso provide B2B options to make this as efficient as possible.

BONUS CHAPTER

AUDIO VOICE
NOTES 101

This chapter is written by someone I regard as the QUEEN of audio voice notes on LinkedIn, the incomparable Holly Allen. I've been working with Holly for several years now and am always blown away at her experience, creativity and success in sending voice notes on LinkedIn and training SDRs to do the same.

This bonus chapter is full of incredible value, and my advice is to read it, digest it and implement *her* advice. I'll add a QR code at the end of the chapter that will link to her LinkedIn profile so you can follow her there.

Voice notes 101

Voice notes will forever be my favourite way to prospect. They are hyper-personalised and make our prospects feel special without being too invasive. You can create so much excitement around what you're saying simply by using energy and intonation in your voice. The real beauty of voice notes is not enough salespeople are using them or even know how to send a voice note, so the ones who do stand out from the crowd and get responses.

Sending a voice note on LinkedIn is pretty simple; the first step is to send a connection request to your prospect, as you cannot send a voice note without being connected. Once they've accepted, you'll need to download the LinkedIn app on your phone if you haven't already. Click on the send message widget, search for the person you want to send the voice note to, and then hold down the record button next to the message box and speak into your phone. A voice note can be up to 60 seconds long, and if you mess up and need to re-record it, simply drag the record button to the left. Once you've sent your hyper-personalised, energetic voice note, like magic, a blue play button will appear in your prospects' LinkedIn inbox. How intriguing—I know!

I'm a big advocate for sending a voice note pretty much as soon as someone has accepted my connection request. This way, you create a sense of urgency, and your name and company name are likely to still be fresh in their mind as you've literally just connected with them. This immediacy will make your prospects feel special, so start the voice note by saying something along the lines of, "Hi *Name*, thanks for accepting my connection request so quickly! I appreciate this voice note is totally out of the blue and you've literally just connected with me, but I'm super-excited to talk to you." It goes without saying, everyone loves to be made to feel special.

The word "special" has come up a lot here—that's because voice notes are for your super-special prospects. Those C-Suite, in-demand prospects that everyone wants a piece of. Chances are, they've already received five cold calls by 10 am, and their email inboxes are bombarded—you've got a pretty good chance of standing out by doing something different and grabbing their attention.

So, you've sent the connection request, they've accepted, and you're getting giddy as you go to send your first voice note. But what do you say?! Enter panic mode. . .

The key to creating a voice note script is that there is no voice note script. This is your chance to be hyper-personalised, showing off your knowledge and research on that prospect and their pain points. You know that phrase in sales, "show me you know me"? Exactly that. Each voice note you send is likely to be different to the one before.

As a rough guide, I'd always open with a welcoming phrase like, "Hi Dan, Holly here from THRIVE. Thanks for connecting with me, and happy Monday!"

Then comes our personalisation. "Dan, I appreciate this voice note is completely random, and you definitely weren't expecting this today, but I saw your recent post on World Mental Health Day and how exercise really helps you. Being an avid runner myself, I had to reach out—running is definitely my happy place, too!"

Then we go into our very (and I mean very) subtle sell: "On the topic of World Mental Health Day, it looks like you're doing a great job over at *COMPANY* with topical campaigns, and I have no doubt you've got your content calendar sorted for the rest of the year. Not sure if you've ever heard of *YOUR COMPANY*, Dan, but we work with the likes of *RELEVANT COMPANY* and *RELEVANT COMPANY* on their campaign strategies to improve employee awareness and engagement on such important events."

And we end with our soft CTA: "I'd love to show you what these pre-built campaigns look like or even have an idea share! Let me know if you'd be up for a virtual coffee sometime soon!"

The key with voice notes is not to use them as an opportunity to have 60 seconds to pitch your product. Make it sound super-conversational, using an upbeat, friendly tone of voice. I'd recommend walking around the room with a natural smile on your face—it will make a difference, I promise.

Say the prospect's name at least twice throughout the voice note. It will keep them engaged and makes it feel even more personalised.

AUDIO VOICE NOTES 101

And try not to read off a script! It's difficult at first, I know, but when we read off a script, we tend to sound like a sales robot. A few "*umms*" and "*ahhs*" are completely okay but try to plan out what you'll say before recording to avoid too many of these.

So, we've sent the voice note—all very exciting. Now what? What if they don't reply? It's definitely achievable to get a response after sending one voice note. In the scenario that they don't respond, wait two days and then follow up with a message along the lines of, "Hey, Dan, appreciate that voice note was super-random ^ haha! Did you have a chance to listen to it? ☺"

And then, if they don't reply to that, wait another two days and go in with a sad meme and a message like, "Was it really that bad, Dan? 😫"

And *voila!* That is voice notes 101.

Disclaimer: Not all of your prospects will appreciate a voice note. I'd always suggest having a look at your prospect's profile first, their persona, their activity, and using your emotional intelligence to determine whether this is going to go down well or not. That said, my experience of sending voice notes and the responses from prospects have by far been the most positive out of all the prospecting channels!

Good luck!

Make sure you follow Holly on LinkedIn to get more incredible insights, tips, strategies and ideas around Sales, SDRs, Social Selling and Audio Voice Notes - https://www.linkedin.com/in/hollyallen1/

PART 6
VIDEO LINKEDIN MESSAGES

CHAPTER 18

VIDEO MESSAGES ON LINKEDIN

I'd like to start this chapter by jumping straight to the elephant in the room and identifying two undeniable truths with video messages. . .

1. They are incredibly effective.
2. They are scary to do for the first time.

Video messages, for most people, are scary. They're scary to record and horrible to watch (who actually likes watching themselves?!). For the first few months that I started recording and sending video messages, I would go out to my car where no one could see, hear or watch me. After recording them, I could never watch them back, as watching myself and listening to myself made me curl up inside.

BUT I saw the value in sending them.

You see, we are all inundated with written messages, written emails and written texts. Video allows people to actually SEE and HEAR us, to see our eye contact and to see our body language. In all fairness, it's the next best thing to seeing them in person. We all know that the same words can be read and interpreted in a number of ways, whereas with a video, not only do you add tone, but you add everything else on top.

Before I run through the steps of how to send them and share my top sales scripts for LinkedIn video messages, I want to run through my top tips for anyone who hasn't yet sent a video message and who might be nervous or uncomfortable doing it.

OVERCOMING THE FEAR OF VIDEO

There are multiple reasons people are hesitant to record and send videos to prospects and customers, including:

- I don't know what to say.
- I don't look good enough for video.
- I don't know how to do it.

- I don't like the sound of my voice.
- I don't have anywhere to record them.

Some may be making additional excuses to themselves, such as "my customers don't like video messages" or "video messages won't work in my industry." If this is you, I hate to say it, but this is probably more in your head than in actual reality—feel free to message me directly if you disagree.

Let's face a few truths, though:

- Video is booming.
- YouTube is a prime example of the power of video.
- Platforms like TikTok highlight the value.
- Zoom/Teams has grown incredibly over recent years.

CHAPTER 19

FROM VIDEO TO SALE IN 24 HOURS

I once created and closed a sale within 24 hours, starting with a personalised video message sent to a prospect. Now, not every video message will convert that quickly! But. . .

Let's start with WHY I sent the video message on LinkedIn in the first place. . .

There are many prompts and reasons to message a prospect on LinkedIn, from seeing them share a piece of content or finding something on their profile to hearing their company make an announcement; the list goes on.

In this situation, a prospect of mine had announced they were starting a new job at a new company.

Now it was the WAY they had announced the new job that prompted me.

They shared a video to announce it!

That made it an easy choice to use a video message to start a conversation.

Now here's an important part of this situation:

I saw their post within five minutes of it being shared BECAUSE I had clicked the new notification bell on their profile, which notifies me every time they post something! This allowed me not only to like and comment on their post straight away but also message before any of my competitors did.

(If you're not already utilising this, click the notification bell on all of your prospects' profiles so you get notified every time they share content!)

Here's where you can find the notification bell:

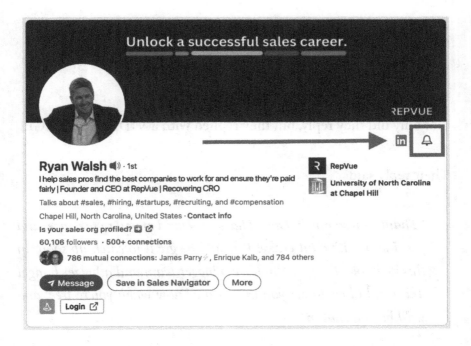

I grabbed my phone straight away, opened up a message and clicked the "Record Video" option on the LinkedIn app.

My message was simply this:

> *"Hey John, HUGE congratulations on the new role. I wasn't expecting this announcement, but I'm so happy for you. You've done so many amazing things at CURRENT COMPANY, and I can't wait to see you do amazing things at NEW COMPANY. I know you're super-busy, but it would be great to catch up soon. It's been way too long."*

No selling. No pitching. Just a heartfelt message.

In under an hour, they replied.

Not only did they reply, but they replied with a VIDEO MESSAGE!

Their reply said:

> *"Thank you so much, Dan. That's very kind of you to message, and yes, I know, it's a bit crazy! It would be great to catch up soon. In this new role, I'm going to have a bigger team and a bigger budget and would love to get you in. Let me know when you're free, and we'll book a chat in."*

Now, at this point, it doesn't make sense for me to reply with a video message because my goal is to book this chat in. So, I replied with a WRITTEN message, highlighting that I had a one-hour gap that day or a few options the following two days.

They replied with a written message saying that today worked, and so the call was booked.

That call lasted 28 minutes, and at the end, we had agreed on what they needed, so I sent the proposal over, and within a few hours, it was sent back signed.

From LinkedIn video message to sale within 24 hours.

Obviously not EVERY video message will turn into a sale or turn into one in under 24 hours.

The key messages I want to convey in this chapter are:

- Video messages are one of the highest-performing forms of prospecting right now.
- With all messaging, the key is hyper-personalisation; make it as much about THEM as possible.
- Speed is CRUCIAL; we are all up against a lot of competition, so reacting as quickly as possible to opportunities is very important.
- Just be human and have human conversations.

CHAPTER 20

TEN VIDEO SALES MESSAGE SCRIPTS

It's worth noting that the video scripts here can work as audio scripts as well and vice versa. The only two differences between them are that with video, you can record up to two minutes, whereas with audio, you can only record 60 seconds—and with video, they can see you!

One of the most important components of an effective video message is to ensure you're looking at the camera and keep strong eye contact (not in a creepy way) and be aware of your body language as well. Your body should face the camera and if you speak with your hands, do that; let them see your passion and energy for what you do.

A few things to consider before recording:

- Your background – Think about what is behind you when you record, and make sure it is tidy and professional.
- Audio & lighting – If you're doing video from your laptop, consider external lighting and a microphone for better quality.
- What you wear – You should be dressed the same way that you would if you were meeting them in person.

VIDEO SCRIPT 1—THE INTRODUCTION

"Anna, it's Dan here from The Daily Sales. I've been a huge fan of Salesforce for a long time and used it a few years ago for my sales team. The Daily Sales is a sales community with over 900,000 salespeople following our page, and we work with companies to help them reach that audience. If you're open to it, I'd love to send you a little more information on how our customers turn those followers into customers. If you're interested, just let me know the best email, and I'll send it over."

NOTE: Make sure you're looking at the camera, smiling and speaking with a positive tone to help them feel comfortable replying to you or coming to you when they're interested if it's not right now.

VIDEO SCRIPT 2—THE WHITEBOARD

Holding whiteboard with their name/company name

"Simon, I'd love to see if I can help you save up to 80% of your recruitment costs this year. We have software here that has helped 165 companies so far reduce their recruitment costs by automating the process and pulling together multiple candidate databases. I noticed at Salesforce you've currently got 27 active roles that you're hiring for, and it looks like you work with a few recruitment agencies as well. If you're open to it, I'd love to send you some more information on what our software does and how it works. If you're interested, just let me know the best email, and I'll send it over straight away."

NOTE: You can buy a whiteboard for minimal cost on Amazon or through an internet search. You can go a step further and doodle/draw their company logo or create something funny or relevant to them.

Try to be creative with what you write on the whiteboard, this is one of the more common forms of video messaging used by salespeople so a lot of your prospects may already be getting whiteboard LinkedIn video messages.

Look for ways that you can stand out or do something a little different (different colours, a joke written down, an observation, etc.).

VIDEO SCRIPT 3—THE RESEARCH REFERENCE

"Hi Ryan, I was just looking through your posts on LinkedIn and noticed a couple of weeks ago that your company RepVue

announced series A funding—congratulations, by the way! I saw in the article that one of the things you were looking to use the funding for was to reach more people and bring on more users. I run a community on LinkedIn called The Daily Sales, which has over 900,000 salespeople following the page. I'd love to see if we could help you drive our followers to become RepVue users. Would you be up for jumping on a call to explore?"

NOTE: Try to ensure that your research reference is RELEVANT. For example, if you're going to reference a funding announcement, make sure you read some articles on the funding to identify what they plan to spend that funding on. Just because a company has received funding, doesn't mean they have cash to burn. Most companies do a press release and often share where the money will go, for example, expanding sales, investing in product development, customer acquisition, etc.

The research needs to be done properly and relevant to them.

VIDEO SCRIPT 4—THE WEBSITE BROWSE

Using Vidyard with their website in the background and your face in a little bubble on the page

"Hi Emma, I was just looking at Lead Forensics' website (which you'll be able to see that I was on!), and noticed that currently you have five active roles for your sales team across the US. We have quite a few candidates who I believe would be a perfect fit and who are ready to interview. They each have a 2–4-week notice period

before being able to start. We put a lot of work into our vetting process and ensure that all our candidates have proven success in their existing or previous roles, which we verify ourselves. If you like, I can send you some information on our process, and if you are interested, I can send these candidates over straight away."

NOTE: When you use platforms like Vidyard and have your prospect's website in your video it takes personalisation to a whole new level, and if you can find something relevant, then it takes relevance to a whole new level.

It could be something on their main page, a press release, job adverts, a testimonial from a company you've also helped or a piece of content. Look for something with the strongest link to what you want to talk to them about.

VIDEO SCRIPT 5—THE LINKEDIN PROFILE VIDEO

Using Vidyard whilst scrolling through their LinkedIn profile

"Hey Tyler, my name is Daniel, and I work at The Daily Sales. I've been following you for a while on LinkedIn and absolutely love what Sales Feed is doing. As I was on your profile today, I noticed about a month ago you joined Sales Feed. I thought it would be worth sending a quick message to ask if you already had a website visitor tracker in place or not. Our software here at Lead Forensics allows you, your marketing team and your sales team to identify which companies are visiting your website and sources their contact details

so you can turn more of those visits into leads and customers. If you are up for it, I'd love to send some information on how it all works."

NOTE: Same as script 4, using Vidyard with THEIR LinkedIn profile in the background takes personalisation to a new level. Relevance is important here as well; there is no point using their LinkedIn profile if there is nothing relevant to reference.

Look through their summary section, their work history, interests, recommendations, endorsements, again anything that has the strongest link to you, your product and/or your company.

VIDEO SCRIPT 6—THE CONTENT REFERENCE

"Darryl, I was reading your post today and wanted to send you a quick message as the story really resonated with me. As someone who counts themself as an introvert as well, it was great to see your post highlighting how this can actually be a superpower in sales. I'm not sure if you've heard of Gong, but we have software that records and analyses cold calls for sales teams. We've found it to be really helpful for introverted sales teams as it takes away the unnecessary pressure of having a manager listen in whilst you make the calls. Would you like me to send you a little more information on what it does and how it works?"

NOTE: This is obviously only applicable if your prospect is sharing content on LinkedIn (which many will be). The beauty of this script is that it gives them a little ego boost by complimenting their content (trust me 99% of people will feel good if you compliment their content). Not only that, it then allows you to tie in something relevant that links to you and your product.

EXTRA NOTE: If your prospect isn't sharing content on LinkedIn, look at other people in their department and within their organisation as there will be some people sharing content and they could be worth engaging with and messaging as a different door into the company.

VIDEO SCRIPT 7—THE REFERRAL

"Hi Harriet. Yesterday I spent the day with Chris and the team at Gong, training them on how to leverage LinkedIn to its full potential. The feedback was brilliant, and after, Chris suggested that I send you a quick message as he thought your team would benefit from the training as well. He said he would message you himself, too, but I wanted to ask if I might be able to send you some more information on what's included in the training and how it could help? If you're possibly interested, all I need is an email address, and I can send some information over straight away."

NOTE: Just mentioning a referral is powerful, but if you can get your customer to send your prospect a message as well, then the impact is greater. Although I do appreciate this isn't always something easy to arrange.

VIDEO SCRIPT 8—THE EXPERT INSIGHT

"Hey Nick, I wanted to send you a quick video as I'm currently writing an article on LinkedIn, which will be titled five big tips

from five software marketing experts, and I would love to include you in it. Given your position as CMO at Cognism and your 20+ years of experience in marketing, I think your tips would be incredibly valuable to our audience. If you're able to spare a few minutes to answer a few questions, I'd love to have you as part of the article. Let me know if you're able to join in, and I'll send over the details."

> NOTE: Eye contact is key in this video to make them feel like you really do want THEM to be a part of your article. Send this to 5–10 of your biggest prospects and not only will you create a fantastic piece of content, but you'll start conversations with a lot of those prospects.

VIDEO SCRIPT 9—THE SIMILAR COMPANY INSIGHT

"Hi Beth, I was speaking to Darryl at Agorapulse yesterday, and he shared something quite interesting that, as a CMO, I thought you might find beneficial. Over there, they are putting a lot of focus into building a media part of the business to compete on social media, something I've seen a few other companies start to do as well. I'm not sure if it's something you've considered at VanillaSoft. Darryl shared a few suggestions on how they were going to do this. Would you like me to send them over?"

> NOTE: This template was actually created after I spoke to a CMO who told me that the one thing they want from salespeople is to be taught something. To be shown what other similar companies are doing that they might not know about.

VIDEO SCRIPT 10—THE THOUGHTFUL GIFT

"Hi Sharon, I saw your post with you and your daughters building Lego sets together, and I honestly thought it was amazing! Our company knows this wonderful place where you can build a custom Lego figure, and we would love to send you a Lego to go with your sets. I just need to know where to send it, and I'll get it made and sent to you straight away. I'm sure it will make a great addition to your city."

NOTE: This template will take some deep researching (which may include venturing outside of LinkedIn and onto Facebook, Twitter, Instagram, TikTok, etc.). But if you can find something about them that connects to a potential gift, then it can be an effective way to build relationships and open doors. It's also worth looking at any podcast interviews they might have done or webinars they might have been a part of as people will usually open up about more things like this during smalltalk.

BONUS CHAPTER

SENDING LINKEDIN VIDEO MESSAGES

This bonus chapter is written by one of the most experienced and successful LinkedIn video experts out there, Jarrod Best-Mitchell. As you'll read below, Jarrod has sent over 6,000 personalised video messages on LinkedIn, and his knowledge and tips are incredibly powerful.

I've known Jarrod for many years, and when I interviewed him for *The Social Selling Podcast*, I was blown away by some of his unique but hugely effective video messaging tips. I hope you enjoy this bonus chapter.

OH, HOW I LOVE SENDING VIDEO MESSAGES ON LINKEDIN!!!

When LinkedIn first introduced the ability to send video messages to your connections back in late 2018 or 2019, I was already heavy into sending voice notes to my new connections, and I saw this as an upgrade and an even better way to build my community on the platform.

To date, I'm proud to say that I've sent close to 6,000 and counting PERSONALISED video messages to my LinkedIn connections. I have seen about a 40% response rate and an immeasurable ROI in terms of my pipeline, my personal brand and engagement on LinkedIn.

Why should you send video messages to your connections?

Even though it has been available for over three years, very few people still send them. VERY FEW. I've gotten less than 50 video messages. Many of the top content creators on the platform also mention that they don't get video messages, so sending a personalised one is a great way to stand out.

Video messages help build community, and that converts your connections into customers.

What is the #1 reason why you would want to do a video? It's personalised, and it lets the receiver know that you took time out of your day to send them that message. As corny as that sounds, it creates a bit of reciprocity with the recipient, and if it's thoughtful, researched and personalised, it will have the impact you want.

Here's what is stopping you from doing video messages to prospects:

Vanity: You're focused on your looks. But think about it; at the end of the day, the receiver must see you one day in person or virtually, so why not do the video now and get over that hurdle? Are you going to show up to the meeting with a bag over your face or the camera switched off?

Not sure what to say: Most people, when they connect with you on LinkedIn, say, "Thanks for connecting." But if you're using the platform to generate business, you want to say something that generates a response, and this is where most people get stuck. As someone who has optimised hundreds of profiles on LinkedIn, clients give me access to their page, and I've seen the messages some people send. . .MOST are AWFUL and have a low response rate. So, it's understandable why most don't do it because they don't see it getting a better response than their current method.

Don't worry. At the end of this chapter, I'll share my framework and structure for sending a great video message.

Automation: There are so many automation tools out there that will help you reach your ideal client with text at the click of a button. I'm not surprised that text is still the go-to for many. Text is easier but, in most cases, not personalised and more likely cut and pasted. Most of the people you're targeting have gotten an automated message in the past, so unless the copy is really, really good, it's unlikely that the message will stand out.

For the few of you who have conquered your fear or reluctance to do video, here are some of the mistakes I see you make.

You say YOUR name: When you send a message to someone on any social media platform, your name is at the top of the message box. So, it's surprising to me that many people repeat their name when it's already there, but I believe that's due to sending a video message like it's a phone call.

The message is too long: 30 to 45 seconds is best for any message. Be specific in your messaging and keep it to one topic/ask.

Look at the camera: Not the screen. Have you ever seen a video where it looks like the person is looking down at you? That's because they're looking at their phone screen instead of the camera. Eye contact is important when sending a video.

Pitching too hard: Don't make your first message a 100% sales pitch. Focus more on determining their interest instead of asking for a meeting.

SENDING LINKEDIN VIDEO MESSAGES

Not looking at their profile: If there's one thing that turns off many on LinkedIn, it's asking a question that is already answered on their profile. What impresses them is referencing to something from their profile.

Untidy background: YES, we have all judged someone based on this. But sometimes, an untidy background can turn off the recipient of your video, so before sending your video, find a clean corner and neutral background, if possible. If you're in an area with a lot of background noise, use captioning tools like CapCut to add captions to your video. Sometimes the receiver is also in an environment where it's not possible for them to listen to your video, but they can most definitely read along with the captions.

Wear your company polo shirt or have it in the background.

Incorporate a whiteboard: Use it and have the connection's name on it.

NOTE: You can only send a video message if you are connected to the person or if they've responded to your InMail message.

We've spent enough time on what's stopping people from posting and the mistakes they make. Now let's focus on best practices.

Here are my top tips when doing videos on LinkedIn.

- <u>Start by saying their name.</u> Don't say good morning or good day. Don't EVER say your name. The best way to get their attention is by saying their name. Think of it as if you called them out on the street. "Hi, Daniel!"
- <u>Wipe your lens.</u> YES. Videos DMs can only be done via mobile or using Vidyard if you're sending while in LinkedIn Sales Nav, so WIPE YOUR LENS. I've seen too many cloudy videos, and as minor as that is, it can be a turn-off for the receiver.
- <u>Incorporate a whiteboard.</u> I got this tip from Vidyard, and it's really helpful. Someone seeing their name on a whiteboard emphasises that it's a personalised message.

Here's when you should send a video message.

I send a video message as the first message to all my connections. After that, I correspond via text or voice, but I use video to create a great first impression.

Videos should definitely be sent to all of your connections; however, if time is against you, ensure you send them to all of your ideal clients.

How soon should you send a video message?

I usually send messages within a week of connecting. I've found that sending it right after connecting with someone can be a turn-off. If it's someone from a company you've wanted to reach, still wait 24 hours after connecting to send the video message.

Video Messaging Script

Standard – *Daniel, thanks so much for making me a part of your LinkedIn network. Really looking forward to engaging with you on this platform.* (9secs)

If you want to, reference to a post they made.

Standard – *Daniel, thanks so much for connecting—your last post about [insert topic] was [insert].* _____.

Mention what resonated and that you look forward to engaging with their content more on the platform.

Connect with a call to action; their name, purpose for connecting, what is the value that I can bring?

E.g., *Hi Daniel, my reason for connecting is because I have been helping small businesses in London (similar to yours) that are concerned about the risk their business is exposed to. The content on my page gives lots of advice on that topic; however, if learning more about that is a priority for you, let me know if you're open to a meeting.*

Don't pitch: e.g., asking for a meeting, pitching your products or services or including your calendar link.

Don't miss out on the opportunity that is video DMs on LinkedIn. Pretty soon, many more people will start doing it, and it will be overused as much as text. It is a great way to cut through the noise with your prospect and will help build your personal brand in the long term.

Make sure you follow Jarrod on LinkedIn to get more incredible insights, tips, strategies and ideas around Sales, Social Selling and Video Prospecting at https://www.linkedin.com/in/jarrodbestmitchell/

PART 7
INMAIL MESSAGES ON SALES NAVIGATOR

CHAPTER 21

INMAIL MESSAGES ON LINKEDIN

For anyone who hasn't used Sales Navigator before, it's a premium platform that LinkedIn offers that works alongside LinkedIn. By paying a monthly fee, you get a whole host of additional features, one being the ability to send messages to people you're not connected with yet. If you hadn't noticed, you cannot do this on standard LinkedIn; you are only allowed to directly message 1st-degree connections—people you are directly connected with.

With Sales Navigator, you are able to send a number of InMail messages to people you are not connected with (the number of InMails you're allowed to send will depend on the level of membership you or your company has).

Now, let me first address the elephant in the room. . .

When someone receives a LinkedIn InMail, they often know one simple truth:

> You have PAID to send them that message. And if you have paid to send them that message, it is probably because you want to or are trying to sell them something!

This puts you at an INSTANT disadvantage when using InMails. They're no different from sponsored ads that you see on most social networks, adverts that companies have paid a lot of money to get in front of your eyes. When you see them, you often are quite quickly put off; it's no different from seeing a salesman approaching you at a shop—you know you're about to be sold to.

So, when decision-makers see an InMail in their inbox, the likelihood is high that they'll be sitting there thinking, "Oh, here we go. Just another sales pitch," to which they'll probably either delete it straight away or ignore it.

DON'T WORRY, THOUGH. . .

Whilst I'm painting a pretty bad picture for InMails, there is hope. They can actually be INCREDIBLY effective when done right, and in this chapter, I'll share all of my secrets to turning InMails into a pipeline and sales.

Let's first look at why many InMail messages DO NOT work. The majority of companies that hire me to train their teams on Sales Navigator often tell me the same thing: the vast majority of the InMails their salespeople send do not get responses. When I say the vast majority, I'd say close to 98–99% don't work. In some companies, it's 100%.

I won't draw this out. I'll tell you exactly why they're not working:

1) They're focused on what the salesperson is selling, not how the prospect will benefit.
2) They're rarely, if ever, personalised. They often just copy and paste templates.
3) They usually ask for more from the recipient than the message gives.

In Chapter 22, I'll share ten tried, tested and proven templates. But first we need to get them to open and read the message, which will have a lot to do with the subject line that you include.

CHAPTER 22

INMAIL SUBJECT LINES

With a standard LinkedIn message that you send to a 1st-degree direct connection, there is no option to include a subject line. However, with InMails to people you're not connected to, you have to add a subject line so that they have some idea why you're messaging and what your message is about.

That subject line has a big impact on whether they open and read your message, so getting it right is crucial. If a prospect gets an InMail and it has a spammy, non-relevant subject line, do you think they'll really want to read it? Given that their phones, email inboxes and LinkedIn inboxes are likely to be FILLED with salespeople try-ing to sell, the need to stand out has never been higher.

The BIGGEST InMail subject line tip. . .

Drumroll. . .

MAKE IT ABOUT THEM!

It sounds so obvious, and yet out of 100 InMail subject lines that I studied, 90% were about the salesperson, the company or the prod-uct, not about me. So, whilst this may seem like an obvious tip, the vast majority of people are simply not doing it.

Within each InMail template that you see in this book, you'll see that it comes with a suggested subject line. Edit these to suit your product or business; they are there to give you an idea of how it should read. Not only that, but at the end of each template, you'll also see a sug-gested CTA (call to action).

The Call to Action is what you would like them to do next, whether it's to send an email address, agree to a call or answer a question. It's important to make sure your CTA is appropriate for the prospect you're messaging and for the template you're using.

Get the subject line and CTA right and pair it with a good template, and you'll be heading in the right direction for more replies and more interested prospects.

CHAPTER 23

TEN INMAIL SALES TEMPLATES

INMAIL TEMPLATE 1—THE EXPERT ARTICLE

SUBJECT LINE: I'D LIKE TO INCLUDE YOU IN OUR ARTICLE

Hi Oscar,

I'm writing an article titled "The Top 10 Expert Marketing Trends for 2023," and I wondered if you would like to share your top trend in it? It will include ten trends by ten marketing experts, and given your extensive experience, I'd love to include you in it. If you're interested, it should only take 5–10 minutes, and I can send over some more detail on the article and what we would need.

I hope you can be a part of it.

Kind Regards,
Dan

TEMPLATE 1 NOTES: This is one of the most effective InMail templates as it not only gives value to the prospect by giving them the opportunity to be in an article, but it also gives you the opportunity to create a great article and then progress the conversation.

IMPORTANT: This isn't just a hollow message; this will only work if you actually write the article (which it is in your best interest to do).

My recommendation is to send this to 5–10 of your top prospects each month/quarter. Use their insights to create one, or a few, articles on LinkedIn. After each one is published, reply to the prospect sharing the link to the article and thanking them for their time, and then progress the conversation. Something like this:

> "Hi Oscar, thank you so much for sharing your insights for our article, here is a link to it – www.linkedin.com/articlelink. I know you're heading up the marketing team at Apple, and I wanted to ask which software you were using for XYZ?"

INMAIL TEMPLATE 2—THE REFERRAL

SUBJECT LINE: DALE DUPREE SUGGESTED I GET IN TOUCH

Hi Christine,

Dale Dupree suggested that I pop you a quick message as he thought you and your team might be looking for LinkedIn & Sales Navigator training. I just delivered a two-day LinkedIn Masterclass to the team at Copier Ninjas, and Dale said that he thought you might be interested in something similar. If you'd like, I'd love to send over a bit more detail on what we cover and what we did with Dale's team.

Kind Regards,
Dan

TEMPLATE 2 NOTES: A key part of this InMail message is to mention the referral's name 2–3 times as this provides more reassurance to the prospect and validity to your product or service. It can also be worth including the results or impact for them of your product/service as well, with either an ROI number or even a bit of text from a recommendation or testimonial from them.

INMAIL TEMPLATE 3—THE STRAIGHT TO THE POINT

SUBJECT LINE: I THINK I CAN HELP YOU SANDRA

Hi Sandra,

I can imagine you get a lot of sales InMail and messages on LinkedIn, so I'll get straight to the point. I think I might be able to save you, and Adobe, up to 80% of your recruitment costs with our system here at RecruitX. I can see you currently have over 30 open roles advertised, so I can imagine saving money on filling them would be worth exploring. If you'd like, I'd love to jump on a quick 15-minute call to show you what we do and to see if it might be beneficial to explore further.

Kind Regards,
Dan

TEMPLATE 3 NOTES: This template only works when the focus is on what's in it for them. There are many "straight to the point" InMails out there that jump into a pitch that's focused on the product, not the solution.

INMAIL TEMPLATE 4—THE ROI NUMBER

SUBJECT LINE: B SYSTEMS MADE AN EXTRA $3 MILLION

Hi Colin,

This year, I delivered a sales kick-off keynote and a 12-week LinkedIn training programme to B-Systems. In the 12 months following, they've accredited an extra $3 million in sales from their team's LinkedIn activity since the training. Given that you are a similar company with a similar size team, I'd love to see if we might be able to help you get more from LinkedIn and grow your sales over the next 12 months and beyond. Would you be open to me sending a little more information on what we cover?

Kind Regards,
Dan

TEMPLATE 4 NOTES: If you don't have a simple ROI number, then look for other ways you can demonstrate the positive impact of your product/service on a customer that you know would also impact the person you are messaging.

INMAIL TEMPLATE 5—THE TESTIMONIAL

SUBJECT LINE: THE BEST SKO KEYNOTE YOU'VE HAD

Hi John,

Richard Kingsley from ABC Software just wrote a testimonial for a sales kick-off keynote that I did for their team, saying it was the best they ever had. The talk covered how their sales team can bring cold calling and social selling together for epic results, and I wondered if you might be looking for a speaker for your next sales kick-off?

Kind Regards,
Dan

TEMPLATE 5 NOTES: If you can try and use a testimonial or recommendation from someone similar to the person that you're sending to, either from a similar company, in a similar industry or in a similar position, this will increase the impact that it will have.

INMAIL TEMPLATE 6—THE FREE OFFER
SUBJECT LINE: FREE CMO EBOOK FOR YOU

Hi Shane,

We've just finished a 160-page eBook sharing insights from some of the world's leading CMOs, which we're offering to marketing leaders today. Would you like a free copy?

Kind Regards,
Dan

TEMPLATE 6 NOTES: The above is a small template example, and you can make it slightly longer, but the goal is to offer them something genuinely relevant and valuable to them, but they need to reply to get it, so you open the door of conversation. This could be an eBook, webinar recording, online course, ticket to an event, physical gift, or anything like that.

INMAIL TEMPLATE 7—THE INMAIL VIDEO

SUBJECT LINE: A SHORT VIDEO FOR YOU SARAH

Using Vidyard to create InMail video

Hi Sarah,

I recorded a short two-minute video for you as I believe we might be able to help *INSERT THEIR COMPANY* both to save money on print costs but also reduce time wasted on errors and fault calls. I've done some research on *INSERT THEIR COMPANY,* which I share in the short video, and if it's something you're potentially interested in, let me know, and I'll send over some more information.

Kind Regards,
Dan

TEMPLATE 7 NOTES: You have an option to just send the video, to which I would recommend reading through the video chapters (Chapters 18, 19 and 20) and perhaps looking at the suggested templates. However, it can also be effective to include a link to a video and then have a template like this that tells them why they might benefit from watching the video. Some decision-makers find videos awkward and don't want to watch them as they have no idea what they contain. By telling them, it helps persuade more to watch it and then hopefully reply.

INMAIL TEMPLATE 8—THE PROBLEM SOLVED

SUBJECT LINE: GET GONG'S SDRS SELLING QUICKER

Hi Devin,

Getting SDRs from start to hitting a number can take time, and that time costs you money. The longer they're not selling, the more they cost you. And that's IF they then hit a number, which we know some won't. We have a solution that can help them start hitting numbers up to one month quicker, and the number can be significant, depending on how many SDRs you hire. Would it be okay to send you some information on how we do this?

Kind Regards,
Dan

TEMPLATE 8 NOTES: The key to this template is to identify, highlight or focus on a common problem your prospect has and how you can potentially solve it. Try not to be assumptive, but share your experience with similar prospects, the problems that they are facing and how you're helping to overcome them.

INMAIL TEMPLATE 9—THE NEW IN-ROLE MESSAGE
SUBJECT LINE: CONGRATULATIONS ON YOUR NEW ROLE, STEVE

Hey Steve,

Firstly, congratulations on your new role at Salesforce! It's quite a change from your last job at Buffer, but I can imagine you're excited for the new challenge. I'm sure you've got a crazy few months ahead of you, but I wanted to reach out as we're working with companies similar to Salesforce, helping them reach more people through their content. Our audience has over 900,000 people, and I wanted to ask if you'd be open to exploring whether there might be opportunities for us to help Salesforce reach them?

Kind Regards,
Dan

TEMPLATE 9 NOTES: Try to dig a little deeper when congratulating them, not just a simple well done! Mention their previous role, mention something about their new company or their team; dig as deep as you can and make it as personal to them as possible to stand out and show that you're keen to help them.

INMAIL TEMPLATE 10—THE COMPANY FOLLOWER

SUBJECT LINE: I NOTICED YOU'RE FOLLOWING OUR COMPANY

Hey Hannah,

I noticed on LinkedIn today that you're following our company, Gong. So, I did a little digging to see if you had worked with us before and noticed that you did two years ago. I wanted to ask if you've considered working with us again? We've had quite a few changes since then. I'd love to jump on a quick call and show you what's new. Or could I email some of them over?

Kind Regards,
Dan

TEMPLATE 10 NOTES: There could be many reasons they follow your company page—perhaps they follow the content, or perhaps they attended a webinar your company ran, etc. Find out first before using it in the message.

PART 8
FOLLOW UP, REPLIES & CONVERTING TO SALES

CHAPTER 24

WHAT IF THEY DON'T REPLY?

No sales strategy works 100% of the time; most work at a relatively low conversion percentage. Cold calling tends to yield a 1–4% success rate, with the majority never turning into anything. With messaging on LinkedIn, you will get people that don't reply at all (if you've worked in sales for more than one day, you'll be used to this!).

So, what happens if they don't reply?

Let me share a quick story of where this really comes to life.

I was booked to deliver training with a company. Whilst doing some final preparation a week before, I noticed someone in my personal LinkedIn network share a post asking for a recommendation for the exact same product that the company I was due to train was selling.

I had a good relationship with the director, so I tagged them in the post, saying that I would personally recommend their company.

The week passed, and the day came when I travelled to deliver their *1-Day LinkedIn Masterclass*. As the team arrived at the training room, one of the delegates approached me and said they had seen the post where I tagged their director. They went on to say that they didn't believe their director had noticed or reacted to it, so they took the proactive approach to comment, connect and message the prospect themselves.

"That's brilliant!" I said. *"What happened next?"* I asked.

"Well, I'm just waiting for them to reply to my message," they said. . .

I paused, looking slightly confused. . .

"I'm sorry, what? You're WAITING for them to reply?"

The room went silent. . .

"*Yes,*" they said, only now starting to doubt their logic.

I went on to explain to them how posts like this easily generate over 100 likes, comments and messages to the prospect. Their LinkedIn inbox will be FULL of messages from salespeople trying to win their business. The likelihood of them replying, unfortunately, is often quite low.

This is one of the biggest missed opportunities in social selling—sitting and waiting for replies.

I can guarantee you that at least 80% of the salespeople that comment on these posts or send LinkedIn messages rarely use other tools as well. They also just sit there and wait; in fact, there is a chance that as you're reading this now, you've acknowledged that you fall into that trap, too. Don't worry if that's the case; we all must learn somehow!

And this is where this section comes into play. . .

What if they don't reply?

Well, if they don't reply, PICK UP THE PHONE!!

Pick up that wonderful phone and give them a call. Wait, what if they don't answer? Well, don't get me wrong, there is also a very low chance that they won't answer your call. If they don't answer, send them an email.

If they don't reply to your email, send them a letter. Then, after a few days, give them a call again. Perhaps try and engage with their content, like a post, write a comment, and let them know that you're there. Keep trying as much as you can.

You need to remember one important thing. . .

YOU ARE A SALESPERSON!

Your job is to hunt—to go out, find, create and close sales opportunities.

Real salespeople don't wait around; they try everything in their power to go out there and help people with their product or service. So, if your prospect doesn't reply to your message, don't wait around. Start using other platforms that are there at your disposal.

CHAPTER 25

PICK UP THE PHONE

Yes, you are reading this right. A LinkedIn book written by a social seller has a chapter called "Pick up the phone"!

I've spent over ten years making, training and leading large sales teams making cold calls. Whilst I now focus on helping salespeople leverage LinkedIn, I know the power and importance of the phone and am certainly not scared to pick it up and use it.

There's an unfortunate stigma in social selling that most social sellers are too scared to pick up the phone and prefer to just hide behind a computer.

Whilst I don't doubt there are people out there scared to use the phone to sell, it's certainly not just social sellers, nor is social selling the reason that salespeople don't use the phone.

It has never been "social selling VERSUS cold calling." Whilst the debate rages on in sales, it's never been about choosing one or the other. Ultimately, if you choose, you lose.

Here's a simple truth that I need you to know:

Some of your prospects will ONLY buy from you if you phone them.

Think back to the modern-day prospecting maze that I showed you in Chapter 2 and what I said about communication preferences. There are many people out there who prefer to use the phone—who prefer to buy or discuss buying over the phone.

This book will hopefully show you how to leverage LinkedIn messaging to generate opportunities and communicate with prospects and customers, but it works EVEN better alongside the phone.

You can use LinkedIn messages to arrange phone calls, generate interest, confirm meetings, send information, follow up, and so much more.

If you fear making cold calls, or if you're trying to justify that they don't work, you don't like them, or they're dead, I would take a minute and challenge yourself.

All you're doing by avoiding using the phone is missing out on a number of potential customers that will only ever buy from you if you use the phone.

CHAPTER 26

CONVERSATION TO OPPORTUNITY

LinkedIn is by far one of the most effective ways to start a conversation with a prospect. As you've seen in this book, there are four ways you can message that will help you start conversations with lots of prospects when done properly.

What is important to remember is that messages on LinkedIn, in any of their forms, are instant messages. In the B2B world, where what you sell is probably not a simple transactional purchase, you'll need to have quite deep conversations. These can rarely be accomplished on LinkedIn alone.

NOTE: It is worth noting that the amount of money people are comfortable spending online grows each year, and so the value of sales that can happen on LinkedIn alone will grow each year as well. I've sold products and services valued between $10,000 and $50,000 via LinkedIn messages alone, and I anticipate those values will grow.

However, most sales conversations that start on LinkedIn will need to leave LinkedIn at some point to continue progressing. These usually progress into an email, phone call, video call or face-to-face meeting.

The key is navigating the conversation and, when the time is right, looking for or creating an opportunity to progress it outside of LinkedIn.

Assuming you've done some level of pre-qualification and you genuinely believe that you can help the person you're messaging, then navigating the conversation shouldn't be too difficult.

It often becomes challenging when you're messaging a complete stranger and hoping for the best!

Now, there will be multiple scenarios that you'll find yourself in when messaging different prospects. For example, some of you will go straight to the point with your initial message, so there will be no need for a fluffy conversation. The message will usually progress outside of LinkedIn after the first reply (for example, if you're asking for a call or an email address to send information).

Other messages will be more conversational, where you will start the conversation discussing something completely different and focus more on building rapport.

You'll then need to look at moving the conversation to one that's connected to what you sell and, more importantly, how you think you might be able to help them.

PART 9
BONUS CHAPTERS

In the first edition of *The Million-Pound LinkedIn Message*, I included several bonus chapters to help provide as many additional Social Selling, LinkedIn and Sales Navigator tips as possible. In this updated version, *The Ultimate LinkedIn Messaging Guide*, I wanted to add even more so you get AS MUCH value from this book as possible!

There are tonnes of tips in these seven Bonus Chapters alone that will help you get more from LinkedIn and social selling alongside sending super-effective messages.

CHAPTER 27

PIPELINE WILL ALWAYS BE KING

From the day the first sale was ever made to the day the last sale is made, one thing will always remain true. . .

Pipeline will always be KING in sales.

Looking back at my time leading sales teams, one of the main reasons for a sales rep missing target was because they hadn't built enough of a pipeline. If you look back at when you've missed your target, how many times would you have actually hit target if you had generated a few more opportunities?

Sales pipelines work like this. . .

Let's say you have to make five sales to hit your sales target. You need to prospect and build a pipeline of opportunities that you work to close at least five to hit target.

The problem is it's not that simple!

Here are some of the common mistakes that salespeople make with their pipeline:

1) THEY DON'T FIND ENOUGH OPPORTUNITIES TO HIT TARGET

A lot of sales reps don't generate enough opportunities each month to hit target. . .

Let's say you need five sales to hit target, as we mentioned above. Unfortunately, salespeople fall into a common trap of only building a pipeline of five opportunities. The reality is that if you build a pipeline of five opportunities, not all five opportunities will close. Which is why many salespeople end up not hitting target.

The key is to understand your close ratio.

If you close 50% of your pipeline, you'll need 50% more to hit target. So, to hit five sales, you'll need at least ten opportunities in your pipeline. If you close 25% of your pipeline, you'll need at least 20 opportunities in order to hit target.

2) THEY LIVE IN PIPELINE DENIAL

Far too many salespeople refuse to accept the reality about their pipeline...

They'll always tell their sales managers that their sales pipeline is amazing, but in reality, it's not. Unfortunately, whilst this attitude will keep their sales managers off their backs, it rarely results in the salesperson hitting target and in the long run, often results in the salesperson struggling.

Pipeline honesty is key to sales success.

If an opportunity has gone cold, if they're not responding to you, if you haven't fully qualified them, anything that makes the opportunity questionable, take it out of your pipeline. Leaving it there will only cause problems.

3) THEY CELEBRATE THE OPPORTUNITY OVER THE SALE

Some salespeople make the mistake of celebrating the opportunity before it becomes a sale...

I've encountered many sales professionals who make SO MUCH noise when they generate a sales opportunity. Now, don't get me wrong, I'm all for celebrating in sales at every stage of the process. The problem is that to a lot of sales reps, that's the peak. They celebrate the opportunity so much that they no longer have the drive to do the follow-up work required to close the sale, and what often happens is the opportunity goes cold.

Pipeline is king, but closed deals are life.

Build your pipeline up with more than enough opportunities, and then make sure you put in the hard work to close as many of them as possible. It's okay to celebrate creating a new and exciting sales opportunity, but true success comes the moment the deal is signed (and the customer is happy!).

4) THEY STOP PROSPECTING WHEN THEY'VE GOT ENOUGH OPPORTUNITIES

Some salespeople spend ages building their pipeline, or they run out of leads and then stop. . .

Now I know it's hard work building a pipeline—it's exhausting! All the efforts required to make loads of calls, send loads of emails, and send loads of LinkedIn messages, along with everything else, is draining. So, when you do finally have enough opportunities, it's easy to want to focus only on converting those. The problem is that each time one closes, your pipeline shrinks.

Building a pipeline is a 24/7/365 thing.

All day, every day, every week, every month, every year; prospecting and building a pipeline should never stop if you work in sales. The best sales professionals out there are prospecting all the time and never stop because they know they need to keep feeding the funnel. For each sale that you close, you need to generate several more opportunities in order to continue closing sales.

This is why pipeline is KING!

No pipeline = no sales.

It's not just "Always Be Closing" in sales; it's also "Always Be Prospecting." You need to keep that pipeline full and work on adding new opportunities all the time.

My top tips:

- Qualify, qualify, QUALIFY – Put as much effort into qualifying your opportunities to make your pipeline as refined as possible. Understand their budget, their timeframe, their urgency, their needs, etc. All this information will massively help your pipeline quality.
- Never stop FEEDING your pipeline – Prospect all the time, make it a habit, and make it a part of your daily routine. Remember, for

each sale you close, you'll need at least 2–3 new opportunities to replace it (as some won't convert).

- Be HONEST with your sales manager and yourself – Pretending that your pipeline is great and you'll definitely hit target will only hold you back. Be honest—if you need help, ask for it. If you need more opportunities, focus on prospecting. If you need help closing, ask for it.
- Celebrate your opportunities AND your sales – Creating a new sales opportunity is an achievement, so be proud of that! But also remember that it's only part of the process. You need to then work on closing the deal to really win.

CHAPTER 28

TEN BIG LINKEDIN & SALES NAVIGATOR TIPS

The best part about LinkedIn and Sales Navigator is that every single month they are continually evolving new features and new strategies.

One of the biggest commitments that I made when I started training LinkedIn & Sales Navigator was to live and breathe it in my own businesses so that I could always bring the latest training to my customers.

Today, I'm going to share the BIGGEST tips of 2022 thus far and what is working best right now.

Let's dig in:

1) SET AN AWAY MESSAGE ON LINKEDIN (SALES NAV TIP)

You will need Sales Navigator or LinkedIn Premium to do this, but it's an amazing feature few salespeople are tapping into. It's your out-of-office auto-reply but built into your LinkedIn inbox.

Let me give you an example of how I used it recently. After announcing a new position as an advisor for a start-up SaaS company (and knowing I would get a lot of congrats messages), I set up the away message to direct people to the company.

Use it whether you're on vacation/holiday, when you've got a busy day, or even just as an auto-response to direct potential customers to a website, piece of content or resource.

2) ADD A COVER STORY VIDEO TO YOUR LINKEDIN PROFILE (LINKEDIN TIP)

Even though it's such a powerful feature, 99% of people that I meet haven't done this yet. You can now record a 30-second video that will sit within your profile photo. This is a fantastic opportunity to tell people who you are and what you, your product or your service do to help.

BONUS TIP: When people first visit your profile, the cover story video will play a four-second preview from the first four seconds of the video. I'd recommend just smiling and even waving at the camera for the first four seconds before speaking.

3) SHARE A TESTIMONIAL POST THIS WEEK (LINKEDIN TIP)

Once or twice a month, it is incredibly valuable to share a testimonial post that will show your network (which should include prospects) the value that you're delivering to customers. This could be in the form of a testimonial, recommendation, case study, or even a text post sharing the results or numbers you achieved for one of your customers.

The key is for this to include REAL numbers, not just a story but tangible results that people can see. Everyone is claiming they can do something, but very few actually show evidence of it.

4) MAKE YOUR SUBJECT LINE ON INMAIL ABOUT THEM (SALES NAV TIP)

When you send an InMail from Sales Navigator to someone you're not directly connected with, you'll need to include a subject line. Just like with emails, subject lines have a big impact on whether someone will open and read your message.

Most salespeople send generic, spammy sales-like subject lines, and the secret is to not make the subject line about you but about THEM.

5) KEEP A RECORD OF THE LINKS OF PROSPECTS' POSTS (LINKEDIN TIP)

When you are researching prospects, you are likely to find key bits in their profiles and also within their LinkedIn activity that will be useful for personalisation and conversation. One of the best tips I teach is to keep records of those findings and posts within your CRM.

I personally use (and recommend using) Pipedrive CRM, and as you can see in the screenshot, it's super-easy to keep notes and include

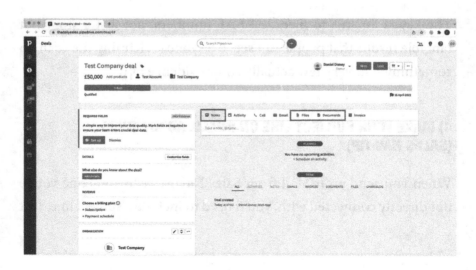

links and key points that you can use throughout the prospecting and sales cycle.

(You can try Pipedrive completely free for 30 days here; it's by far the best CRM out there.)

6) SEND A VIDEO MESSAGE TO ALL CURRENT PROSPECTS (LINKEDIN & SALES NAV TIP)

From my experience, having worked with thousands of salespeople and speaking to C-Level decision-makers worldwide, roughly 99% of salespeople are NOT sending video messages on LinkedIn.

Not only does this make those who do stand out, but because they are so engaging, they are converting incredibly well. I'd highly recommend sending a video message to any and every prospect you haven't already sent one to. Make sure each one is recorded personally, look at the camera and be genuine.

7) ADD A LINK TO YOUR LINKEDIN PROFILE (LINKEDIN TIP)

A new feature on LinkedIn now allows people to include a clickable link to their LinkedIn profile. This gives you an amazing opportunity to direct people to your company website, a resource, a webinar, or anything you think might give them value and start them or progress them on the journey to hopefully work with you.

8) START A NEWSLETTER (LINKEDIN TIP)

Again, I try hard to live and breathe everything I teach, and you're literally taking part in that right now with this tip! Newsletters are one of the highest converting forms of content on LinkedIn currently, which is why I have two and write them regularly.

These are exactly the same as articles published on LinkedIn, but people can subscribe to them. When someone subscribes to a newsletter, LinkedIn notifies them each time you share a new one, helping you reach your target audience more effectively and give value to them. (*Hopefully, you're getting value from this newsletter today!*)

9) SHARE A PHOTO OF YOURSELF TO HELP PEOPLE GET TO KNOW YOU (LINKEDIN TIP)

Sharing pictures of yourself can be scary at first, but it's extremely valuable. You want your audience, prospects and customers to get to know you. Let them see you at work, let them see you outside of work, and let them get to know you as a real person, not just another corporate bot.

It can be anything from a selfie at your desk (home or office) all the way to a picture on your wedding day (yes, that's me a few weeks ago getting married in Florida!).

10) CHECK YOUR PROFILE VIEWS (SALES NAV TIP)

There is a reality that few salespeople consider: Some of your IDEAL prospects are viewing your LinkedIn profile, and if you're not checking, you are missing a HUGE opportunity to speak to them.

With standard LinkedIn, you can see the most recent four or five, but with Sales Navigator or premium LinkedIn, you can see EVERYONE. Scroll through them daily, look for people that match your ideal customer persona, and then send them a message like this:

"Hi Sarah, thank you for taking a look at my profile today! I'd love to know how your sales team is currently using LinkedIn."

Kind Regards,
Dan

CHAPTER 29

SOCIAL SELLING TOP TIPS

1) CREATE YOUR OWN BILLBOARD LINKEDIN PROFILE BANNER

You waste a valuable opportunity if you are not utilising LinkedIn's profile banner. Most salespeople either leave it blank or with a bland, generic or corporate image. The reality is that this is the perfect space to have your own personal billboard! It's one of the first things your prospects will see, and so it's a great opportunity, in as few words as possible, to tell them what you offer.

2) HAVE AN ELEVATOR PITCH STYLE PROFILE SUMMARY

Most of us know the elevator pitch principle: the idea that if you were in an elevator with a prospect, what would you say in 30 seconds that would tell them what it is you do and give them a reason to be interested? Well, your LinkedIn profile summary is now your modern-day digital elevator pitch.

It's often the first thing people will read and learn about you. My top tip is to make it customer-focused; don't write about how great you are at selling but write about how great you are at helping people.

3) COMMENT ON RELEVANT POSTS EVERY SINGLE DAY

You don't need to spend more than 5–10 minutes per day commenting on at least 2–3 posts to make an impact. Make sure the posts you comment on are industry relevant.

Some may be posts shared by your prospects; some may be posts shared by key industry people or other people that work in your prospects' company. Those comments will help build your personal brand and get your name known to your prospects, making for warmer introductions.

4) WRITE A POST EVERY SINGLE DAY

This shouldn't take any more than 5–10 minutes each day but is one of the quickest and best ways you can build a personal brand and generate sales opportunities. The posts should be valuable to your prospects and network. You can tell stories, share experiences, ask questions or start debates—use it as an opportunity to give value to your audience and open the doors to you. Let them see and get to know you as a real human being.

5) SHARE VIDEOS ON LINKEDIN

Recording and sharing a video on LinkedIn isn't the easiest thing to do; trust me, when I started recording videos of myself, it was one of the toughest things I've ever done! I used to hate holding my phone in front of my face and talking to myself for a few minutes—it was even worse watching it afterwards.

However, video is one of the most powerful forms of content on LinkedIn, and it's growing every day. Try sharing a few videos each month, no more than 2–3 minutes each with subtitles/captions, on valuable content for your prospects.

6) CUSTOMISE YOUR LINKEDIN PROFILE URL

Another super-simple but effective tip is to customise your LinkedIn profile URL code. When you set up your profile, it will automatically give you a URL that will be full of random numbers and letters, which isn't easy to share. If you go into your profile and look at the top right-hand corner, you should see the option to "Edit Public Profile & URL."

Click that, and at the top right-hand corner of that page, you'll see the option to edit your URL. For example, mine is: www.linkedin.com/in/danieldisney.

7) ADD A LINK TO YOUR PROFILE IN YOUR EMAIL SIGNATURE

This is such a simple but powerful tip. Add a link to your LinkedIn profile to your email signature. You can just write the link in, or it's pretty easy to add in a LinkedIn logo that links through (just search Google for LinkedIn email signature).

It means that everyone you email (which I'm sure are tonnes of people!) will be directed to your profile. This will help you grow your audience and potentially help you grow relationships with prospects and customers.

CHAPTER 30

BUILDING A STRONG LINKEDIN PROFILE

Most salespeople when going into a customer-facing environment, whether it's a face-to-face meeting, a skype call or a networking event, will dress as smart as possible.

They'll put on nice suits, dresses, shoes, jewellery, accessories, hair, make-up, etc. They'll make a significant effort to look their best for their prospects or customers to make a good impression.

What you don't see is business and sales professionals have the same attitude towards their social profiles.

We now have both a physical and DIGITAL presence to consider. We not only have to look presentable physically but we should apply that same logic to our digital presence—our social media profiles and personal brands.

Here's a little doodle I did to illustrate it. . .

The reality is that there are probably more prospects and customers looking at your social profiles than looking at you face-to-face. Your social profile should look as good as you do, and you should invest just as much time as you would in your physical appearance.

With that in mind, here are the basic steps necessary to create a strong LinkedIn profile:

Before we jump into each section, one thing to always remember with your LinkedIn profile is to think about your target audience.

If you're trying to get a job, for example, then your profile should be all about why someone should interview or employ you. If you're looking to prospect and sell through LinkedIn, then your profile needs to be all about the value you offer.

The way to look at it is to imagine your dream prospect visiting your page right now. What would you want them to see to feel comfortable talking to and potentially buying from you? Every part of your profile should be built to help your prospect get to know and trust you to then give you the opportunity to progress that relationship.

Let's break down each section of your LinkedIn profile. . .

Profile Photo: Let's start with one of the most important components of your profile: your profile picture. I've seen some great and not-so-great ones over the years. I know it's not always easy finding a suitable smart photo to use, which is why I often see photos from weddings (often the last time a nice photo was taken when you were dressed smartly!).

The reality is that most people reading this now have a smartphone with a pretty powerful camera, so next time you're in the office, get a colleague to take a decent headshot against a plain background, and boom, perfect profile picture!

Background Image: Behind your profile photo is space for a background image to be loaded. Please don't ignore this part; it's fine to choose a plain background or upload a generic one, but you can create a custom one for free using Canva (www.canva.com). You can include your company logo or mission statement or even your contact details. Something that looks smart, looks on-brand, and captures attention.

Headline: The next step is the headline. This is often just populated with your job title, which is fine; however, you can be a little more creative and make it more about what you do or what you can offer. For me, I use LinkedIn to grow my personal brand, so my headline talks about me, but you might want to discuss what you offer or a reason or how you can help your target customer.

Summary Section: This section is your opportunity to give a nice elevator pitch summary of you, what you do and what you can offer. Mine highlights a summary about me, what I can offer, achievements that help prove my ability to deliver and my contact details. I realise your contact details are available on your profile, but you should want them to be as clear as possible, so popping them into the summary box helps make them even more visible.

TOP TIP: *You can attach media to your summary and work experience. This can be an image, blog, video, website, presentation or link and is a great way to provide some extra media, highlighting what you offer.*

Articles & Activity: This will show all your activity, as in posts you like, comment on, or share. This section will also show the articles/blogs that you write on LinkedIn. This is another place your prospect may look, so it's important to be aware of what content you like and how you engage as your prospects may see it.

Work Experience: This section is for you to list your past and current work experience. Less is often more in these sections, but give your prospect the opportunity to see what experience you have and how it may relate to your ability to provide value to them.

This is also a good place to include a little more about your current company and what makes it different/unique. There is also the ability to add media, so you can link the company website, include your sales pitch presentation or a video—any media that will help the prospect buy into what you do.

Featured Skills & Endorsements: This is one of the real stand-out features of LinkedIn as both a fantastic recruitment platform and a fantastic sales platform. In this section, potential buyers can see areas where you are endorsed by other people.

For example, if you were selling software and your prospect could see you were endorsed for "Software," "Account Management," "Customer Service," etc., by plenty of people, it helps them feel more comfortable buying from you.

Recommendations: Taking it one step further, not only can people endorse you for skills, but they can write a full personal recommendation! Imagine again that you're selling software and your prospect visits your profile, seeing there are several recommendations from other software companies talking about how much you helped them, saved them money, listened to them, etc.

TOP TIP: *Just as I'm sure you'll have a referral process in place to get referrals and case studies from your customers, create one to get recommendations on your LinkedIn profile, as they are just as powerful.*

Accomplishments: This is a great opportunity to list any courses, certifications or awards that you've received. Again, imagine your prospect viewing your profile and being able to see what you are qualified in. It adds some real power to how you are seen.

Interests: You might not think this would interest a prospect, but imagine they looked at this part and saw that you were interested in key industry companies or pages. It would show them that you're interested in what they are interested in.

EXTRA Quick Profile Tips
- Keep it up to date; make sure you're updating it regularly.
- Create a simple, personalised link for your LinkedIn profile.
- Add that link to your email signature.
- Include the link on your business cards.

Follow these tips, fill in each section, make sure it flows nicely and looks professional, and at every stage, make sure you think about how your customer will feel reading it. Will it scare them off, or will it make them want to talk to you and feel comfortable buying from you?

CHAPTER 31

COLD CALLING IS LIKE BLOCKBUSTER

I've talked a bit about cold calling in this book, and hopefully, you'll see that I'm very pro–cold calling, unlike some social sellers who take an anti–cold calling approach.

So, why Blockbuster? Is it because it went bust? Am I saying cold calling is dead? NO!

Actually, in my opinion, Blockbuster should still be alive and thriving today in the same way that a lot of cold callers are thriving.

What Blockbuster highlights is change and how refusing to change or adapt is a risky way to approach business. Blockbuster ended as a business because it didn't adapt quickly enough to evolve with the rest of the industry. Whilst new businesses were coming up with streaming services, which were growing fast, Blockbuster refused to adapt and kept pushing the "film rental" market.

Technology advanced, and people were able to watch films on demand—when they wanted with no late fees!

Now, if Blockbuster had adapted and launched a streaming service, they could still be going (and growing) today. Blockbuster had a huge brand known all over the world for films, and they could have easily built and grown a streaming brand in the same way Netflix has. They could have kept the stores going as people still like to shop and would still rent newly released movies that aren't available on Netflix or streaming sites.

This is EXACTLY the situation that cold calling is in right now!

Cold calling is a prospecting activity that thrived when the phone was our main source of communication. Just like Blockbuster thriving when the only way we could watch films was to buy or rent them via video or DVD.

The same way the world of streaming and downloading interrupted the film industry, other forms of communication, such as social media, instant messaging, email and video, are now interrupting the prospecting and sales industry.

If you refuse to adapt and evolve, if you think the phone will always be the main form of communication and that nothing will change, there is a high probability that you will end up like Blockbuster—out of business.

I'm not saying that the phone will die. Like I said at the start, people still buy and watch DVDs in the same way people still use and will continue to use the phone for years to come. However, people are now communicating more via social media, instant messaging, email and video. Now is the time to adapt to these new methods, learn them properly and master them.

Blockbuster, Toys "R" Us, it's the same story. . .

In the UK a few weeks ago, it was announced that Toys "R" Us, a popular toy shop, was closing down. Most people jump on this to blame websites such as Amazon, which certainly contributes to this.

However, in the same way Blockbuster could still be thriving today, so could Toys "R" Us! If they had adapted to the changing way that people buy and embraced the online world of purchasing, they could still be thriving.

The salespeople and sales teams that embrace social selling, email, messaging and video are thriving today. They've grown their pipelines, increased their sales and grown their businesses. Suddenly, they're able to reach more people and have more conversations.

What should you do?

If you are ONLY cold calling, now is the time to really wake up to the fact that this is not a strong sales strategy. You're missing out on loads of opportunities to generate sales via social media, email, video and instant message. It's not about replacement but utilising it ALONGSIDE cold calling.

The phone will continue to be a strong source of prospecting, but there are A LOT of people using or who are more responsive to other platforms. Be smart, be proactive and use them all!

CHAPTER 32

SOCIAL SELLING IN 15 MINUTES PER DAY

Salespeople are busy. Fact.

Between making hundreds of cold calls, attending countless team meetings, sending emails, sending proposals, closing deals, overcoming objections, and the list goes on they are indeed busy!

When you then have people telling you that you should be social selling now as well, where on earth are you going to find the time to do that?!

Are you really supposed to spend hours each day on LinkedIn?

Luckily, the answer is no!

In this chapter, I want to show you how you can achieve social selling results in as little as just 15 minutes each day. Surely everyone reading this can find 15 minutes each day. Especially if those 15 minutes have the potential to generate you MORE sales?

But Dan, there's no way I can achieve anything in just 15 minutes!

I actually mentioned this on a webinar recently, and a couple of the attendees pushed back and said that wasn't possible. Don't get me wrong; if you can and want to invest more time into social selling, you'll obviously have the opportunity to generate more results.

However, as many salespeople and sales leaders are often crazy-busy as it is, I wanted to find a way that, with as little time as possible, they could find a better way to leverage LinkedIn and start generating results.

Let me show you how. . .

To really see results, I've broken the 15 minutes into three five-minute activities. To see results, the activities need to occur on a regular, consistent daily basis. That's part of why this works.

1 – Grow Your Network (Five minutes)

The first stage is to start growing your network each and every day. Spend the first five minutes adding potential prospects, adding people within prospective companies or adding people relevant to your industry. LinkedIn automatically recommends people for you, or you can do a couple of quick searches.

If you can add at least ten connections each day, that's 300 each month and 3,600 in a year. If you're slowly filling your network with prospects, you'll then increase the chance of generating inbound enquiries, plus you'll create the opportunity to start outbound conversations with them via messaging.

2 – Share & Create Content (Five minutes)

Five minutes isn't a lot of time in the world of content, but it's enough to start. My advice is to subscribe to as many industry-relevant channels as possible. This way, every day you'll get the latest industry news direct to your inbox. Finding a good article and clicking the LinkedIn icon to share takes a couple of minutes, plus adding your own thoughts takes you up to five.

Creating a nice post can easily be done in five minutes. Whether it's a quick photo of yourself in a specific location with some writing attached, a quick story, some insight or even a short three-minute video, you can easily create something impactful in five minutes. My advice is to share two bits of news and create three posts each week.

By sharing content every day, you'll first start to build a personal brand. Done right, your content has the potential to generate inbound leads, and you have the opportunity to use the engagement or content to start conversations with prospects.

3 – Social Post Engagement (Five minutes)

The final five minutes should be invested in social engagement. This includes everything from liking a few posts to commenting on a few posts. This should be a mixture of engaging your prospects' content but also industry-relevant content.

The aim is to make sure your name is out there every day. By engaging on your prospects' posts you'll earn credibility, build relationships and hopefully generate opportunities. By engaging in industry-relevant posts, you'll start to build your personal brand, which will be noticed by prospects and peers.

And there it is, three simple five-minute activities, just 15 minutes per day, that, done regularly, have the potential to generate some pretty rewarding results.

Now you could spend 20 minutes a day, 30 minutes, or more. The key is to make sure you're INVESTING and not wasting that time.

CHAPTER 33

THE ABC'S OF SOCIAL SELLING

The movie, "Glengarry Glen Ross" featuring Alec Baldwin, created the now-popular sales phrase:

"Always Be Closing"

His speech to motivate the team to stop waiting around for sales and instead focus on getting them the buy has helped plenty of sales professionals over the years. This was actually a very effective approach in the past, where selling required more push.

To be fair, closing sales is still a big part of sales success.

Unless you close the sale, there is no sale; everything else means nothing until the deal is done. However, the way we close and, in fact, the way we sell has changed over the years.

Part of that change includes the introduction of social media into the sales process.

Social Selling is quite simply the effective use of social media in the sales process. Sales professionals can use social media to find, connect and communicate with prospects and customers in the same way they might use the phone, email or face-to-face.

With people now spending more time on social media every day, it has become a crucial platform to help salespeople reach more people and enhance the way they sell.

There are key fundamentals to achieving success with social selling. Many salespeople spend a great deal of time on social without generating many, if any, results. It's the same as those sales professionals who don't know how to cold call effectively, making hundreds of calls every day with no results in the end.

The key is to learn how to do it properly.

To help, here are the ABC's of Social Selling that focus on the core fundamentals:

1) Always Be Connecting

The first ABC of Social Selling is to *Always Be Connecting*. Effective social selling comes from your ability to find and connect with potential prospects and customers. The more prospects and customers that you have in your network, the more opportunities you'll have to generate in the short and long term.

> Top Tip: There are many great methods for prospect searching on LinkedIn, but when actually connecting with people, it's often worth making the effort with your LinkedIn connection request. Nothing too sales-rich, just simple and light. To bring this tip to life, set yourself a goal to connect with X amount of new people every single day. It could be five; it could be ten. Whichever number works for you.

2) Always Be Creating Content

The second ABC is to *Always Be Creating Content*. Successful social sellers create engaging and great personal content to share with their network of prospects and customers. Their content helps showcase their expertise, build trust and start the all-important sales conversations.

> Top Tip: Your content shouldn't be about your product but should be about YOU and your thoughts/knowledge/expertise. Create content such as posts, blogs, videos and images that offer value, insight and knowledge, which then draws people to your profile and website, where you can leverage that to start conversations.

3) Always Be (Starting) Conversations

One of the most important fundamentals and ABC number three is to *Always Be (Starting) Conversations*. Social media is fun and likes and followers make us feel popular and important. But they certainly don't equate to pipelines and revenue until you turn them into REAL conversations that become meetings, pitches and presentations.

> Top Tip: When you share great content and you get likes and comments, use them to start conversations via messenger. It might be a thank-you or an opportunity to further discuss the topic. If they are qualified prospects, those conversations can then potentially be worked into sales conversations.

4) Always Be Consistent

The last ABC is to *Always Be Consistent*. Social Selling success comes from this on a daily basis. For example, if you only cold call someone once and they don't answer, that's it. It's the same if you participate in some social activity but then don't for a period of time—the results won't come. You need to build it into your sales process and do it every day.

> Top Tip: Set time aside every single day to do social selling activities. You could devote 15–30 minutes at the start of your day to connect with people, send messages and write a post. You may then touch base at lunchtime to do the same and again at the end of the day. Set your calendar to ensure that time is focused on socials.

And there they are, my ABC's of Social Selling!

PLEASE LEAVE AN AMAZON REVIEW!

I truly hope that you have enjoyed reading this book and that you're able to use it to generate more results from LinkedIn.

If you did enjoy it, I would be extremely grateful if you could spare five minutes to write a review on Amazon. It would be a huge help to me and would also help *The Ultimate LinkedIn Messaging Guide* reach as many people as possible.

As a thank-you, if you are able to spare some time and write a quick review, I would love to send you some recorded LinkedIn training webinars and some LinkedIn eBooks that I share with my customers.

Simply pop me an email at danieldisney@thedailysales.net with a screenshot, and I'll send them straight across.

Thank you!

Daniel Disney

WORKING WITH DANIEL DISNEY

I f you, your business or your sales team want to increase the number of leads and sales that they generate from LinkedIn, then Daniel is the man to call.

INTERNATIONAL KEYNOTE SPEAKER

Daniel Disney is one of the most in-demand and award-winning sales speakers, bringing unrivalled energy and passion to the stage, and inspiring audiences around the world. Daniel lights up stages

Jim Skelly · 1st
VP INTL SALES at CAMBRO
3m · ...

Fun memory! Great investment in social selling training! Daniel Disney we probably gained USD $2-$3million in new business in 2020 and 2021 because of DD's training.

FIGURE 3

at sales kick-offs, corporate sales events, expos and business conferences, as well as delivering highly engaging virtual talks and keynotes. By leveraging modern, social, and digital sales tactics to improve and increase sales, Daniel motivates and inspires businesses, sales leaders and salespeople.

> *"Dan lit up the stage, delivering an outstanding, power-packed keynote presentation full of enthusiasm and passion about the amazing potential when using LI properly for social selling. He explained the WHY and the opportunity everyone was missing by not doing it, and he broke it down into easy-to-understand concepts for our global sales team and distribution partners, representing 35 countries."*

Jim Skelly—VP International Sales at Cambro

Daniel delivers a variety of talks on LinkedIn on Social Selling, Digital Selling, Personal Branding, Sales Motivation, Sales Leadership and more.

LinkedIn, SOCIAL SELLING, SALES NAVIGATOR & PERSONAL BRANDING TRAINING

Daniel Disney is one of the world's leading LinkedIn and social selling trainers. He helps businesses and sales teams leverage LinkedIn and social media to their full potential as a lead-generating and sales-generating machine.

His hugely popular 3- to 12-month social selling programmes, LinkedIn & Sales Navigator Bootcamps and Masterclasses have been delivered to FTSE 500 companies and SMEs all around the world. They cover all aspects of social/digital selling, helping teams to master LinkedIn and to begin generating more results from it.

Daniel also delivers Personal Branding Workshops and Content Masterclasses, as well as offers LIVE Virtual Training and an On-Demand Online LinkedIn Course.

Consulting & Advising

Working with Founders, C-level executives, business owners, authors and experts, Daniel provides consulting and advisory services, helping you and your business become the top on LinkedIn.

For more details, head to www.danieldisney.online, or to enquire about Daniel speaking at your next event or training you or your team, email danieldisney@thedailysales.net.

WHAT DANIEL'S CUSTOMERS SAY:

After reading Dan's book, I was so excited about everything he explained about social selling that I bought 25 copies for our key sales managers.

I was convinced about Dan's best practices on social selling that he lays out perfectly in his book. Sending the book out to the sales team didn't get the "buy-in" or adoption that I was hoping for, so I hired Dan to give a one-hour keynote speech at our 2020 International Sales Meeting that was held in January in the Philippines.

Dan lit up the stage, delivering an outstanding, power-packed keynote presentation full of enthusiasm and passion about the amazing potential when using LI properly for social selling. He explained the WHY and the opportunity everyone was missing by not doing it, and he broke it down into easy-to-understand concepts for our global sales team and distribution partners, representing 35 countries.

On the second day of the meeting, Dan went deeper and taught four one-hour, hands-on workshops to get everyone comfortable with the opportunities on LI. He successfully eliminated the fear factor, built confidence, and explained the ABCs of proper social selling, best practices, Dos and Don'ts and the importance of taking consistent daily action. He was well worth the investment, and I believe he convinced 120 international salespeople to get on board with social selling. We will be hiring Dan again this summer to teach another class to our EMEA sales team, so nobody backslides.

**Jim Skelly—Vice President of International Sales,
Cambro Manufacturing**

I cannot praise Daniel highly enough.

Daniel's Social Selling Masterclass was an extremely useful learning exercise for our team. He had extensive knowledge of possible techniques that could be applied to our business and provided exceptionally detailed training and insight on social selling, which we were able to put into practice immediately.

Daniel's attitude and personality were exemplary. He displayed a good knowledge of the subject and built up a rapport with the attendees in no time. Daniel was a brilliant tutor, had an excellent quality of delivery, a depth of knowledge and also communicated really well with all delegates. Pacing, delivery and passion for the subject and level of knowledge were/are excellent.

Our team thoroughly enjoyed this course and learned a great deal from the day spent at our HQ.

We thought the Masterclass was worth every penny and will certainly use him again.

Thank you again, Daniel, and keep up the great work you're doing in this space.

Tim Johnson—CSO at Visualsoft

Daniel spent the day with our sales, marketing, product, and IT teams and delivered his LinkedIn training course, which was even better than I anticipated! Daniel connects with his audience, tailors his content to suit, and even managed to perfectly engage a US team member who attended via video chat.

Daniel's knowledge, experience and overall approach work impeccably well. I would recommend Daniel to anyone wanting to understand the power of socials, and I'd encourage you NOT to reserve his expertise to just sales as "everyone works in sales!"

Luke Warren—Chief Executive Officer at Kinetic

If Social Selling is your game, then Daniel Disney is the name you need to know!! A fantastically engaging and insightful workshop. Daniel really knows how to help you get the most from it!

Every member of our team got something worthwhile from it, and within days, we have all been trying new techniques and venturing into the seemingly scary world of blogs and vlogs (it's not as scary as it first seems!)

I cannot rate Daniel's workshop highly enough, and it is a must for anybody looking to improve their social media performance.

Gavin Dawson—Managing Director at CamAce Ltd

I would thoroughly recommend Daniel and his sessions on social selling. I recently attended one of his sessions and, since then, have seen a huge improvement in my use of social media.

After a few tentative attempts at interesting and engaging posts, I seemed to hit a note with people and had over 4000 views on a simple picture. I don't have anywhere near 4000 connections. My profile views jumped by over 700%, and I have had many connection requests.

Graham Cameron – Barclay Communications

I recently attended Daniel's "Social Selling Masterclass." Daniel has been there, seen it, done it! His workshop was excellent, with his incredible experience and insights shared alongside dispelling some common myths about social media selling.

Daniel's enthusiasm, energy and experience were apparent during the day. I have implemented the learnings, and results are coming in (on some prospects that I've been targeting for over nine months!)

If you get the chance to attend this workshop, you will not regret the investment. Daniel is one of the best social media experts I've had the pleasure of meeting and working with.

Ian Beighton – Senior Vice President Business Development and Sales EMEA at Innovecs

I first met Daniel at the Sales Innovation Expo and had the pleasure of working with him as he was a Keynote Speaker for my show, and his Keynote was one of the most attended of the show.

His dedication and diligence to his profession are a testament to the company he has built from scratch. I feel I have learned a lot from him in regard to Social Selling and look at him as being at the forefront of the Social Selling Revolution.

Gavin Harris – Director of B2B Marketing Expo

I have been following Daniel for years, soaking up all his content published on LinkedIn. When he wrote his first book, I bought it immediately and saw success very quickly. I recently contacted Daniel to run a Social Selling Master-class for Fivetran. From the first contact, he was a pleasure to deal with. Our BDRs & AEs got so much value from this session. Although it was online due to covid, Daniel's enthusiasm and delivery had us engaged from the first minute. I would highly recommend Daniel to any sales/business development leader who cares about social selling! Thank you, Daniel! (The book delivery was an extra special touch!)

Alison McCabe – Director of Business Development EMEA at Fivetran

ACKNOWLEDGEMENTS

There is a great quote:

> "If the people around you don't lift you up, then you don't have a circle of friends, you have a cage."
>
> — Unknown

I am very fortunate to have amazing people around me who have helped me throughout my life, and I work hard to make sure I surround myself with the best people that I can. I'd like to acknowledge them as being influential in everything I do now and in writing this book.

Firstly, I want to thank my amazing wife, Laurie. I wouldn't be who I am today or be doing what I do if it wasn't for you. Laurie helped me years ago and keeps my ego in check. Working and

ACKNOWLEDGEMENTS

being successful in sales and entering the world of social media can have a huge impact on your ego. Laurie has helped me remember what's important in life and the importance of keeping grounded. Whilst it is important to celebrate success and be proud of your achievements, success isn't a destination, it's a journey. I would like to say a big thank-you to our two wonderful sons, too, Joshua and Lewis. Everything I do, I do for you both. To try and provide you with opportunities that I didn't have, to provide you with experiences and memories, to help you as much as I physically can to set up a good future for you. I am so immensely proud of the men you are both becoming, and thank you for being a constant source of motivation for me.

I'd also like to say thank you to my nan and grandad, two of the biggest inspirations in my life. They taught me the importance of hard work and determination and the importance of family. I spent a lot of my childhood with them, and they were the centrepiece of our family. They worked so hard throughout their lives to provide for their children and their grandchildren. Every day I work hard to build a future for my family as they did for theirs.

To my dad, who taught me both humour and creativity. My dad is the best artist that I know and pushed me to be creative as often as I can. He also has the best sense of humour, and bringing those together with my passion for sales helped me create and build *The Daily Sales*.

ACKNOWLEDGEMENTS

To my mum, for when you would listen to me as a child talk about my many dreams of starting my own businesses and being successful. You listened, you challenged, and you guided me.

To my Uncle Al and Auntie Kim, for how you have always pushed me to be the best I can be. Uncle Al, you will always be the person who guided me into sales and supported me through my early sales roles. I wouldn't have achieved the success I have in sales were it not for you.

To my sister Yasmin, for how you've always inspired me to dream big but always have fun along the way. No matter what, you've always been there, as I will always be for you.

To Nikki and Geoff, for how you took me into the family from day one and have been supportive and guiding in helping me achieve my dreams of building my business. Thank you for being there for me, Laurie, and the boys, and thank you for the holidays and roasts.

To my best friend, Croly. Your entrepreneurial aspirations inspired me when we were just 16 and running our own little eBay businesses. We've shared successes, failures, laughs and many, many memories.

Thank you as well to Annie and the team at Wiley for all your support and help during the writing of this book.

I'd also like to say a big thank-you to the amazing people I'm honoured to have in my professional circle as my peers, colleagues and as my friends: Chris Murray, Dale Dupree, Alex Goldfayn, Gavin Ingham, Steve Burton, Karen Dunne-Squire, Darryl Praill, Benjamin Dennehey, Devin Reed, Niraj Kapur, Alison Edgar, Stu Heinecke, Scott Barker, Mark Jung, Paul Fifield, Ben Wright, Jim Skelly, Jeb Blount, Tony J Hughes, Will Barron, Holly Tripp, Tyler Lessard, Zoe Pepper, Lee Bartlett, Tony Goodchild, James Ski, Ian Gribble, Tony Morris, Vedran & Mirela, Scott McNicholas, Nazma Qurban, Ed Armishaw, Shane Burchett, and everyone else that I can't fit in (but who hopefully know who they are!)

FINALLY, THANK YOU TO YOU, THE READER.

Thank you for buying this book, and thank you for reading it. I not only hope you enjoyed it but that it helps you get more from LinkedIn.

Please feel free to follow me on LinkedIn & Twitter for regular content on LinkedIn, Social Selling and Sales:

LinkedIn: https://uk.linkedin.com/in/danieldisney

Twitter: @thedandisney

ACKNOWLEDGEMENTS

If you have any questions at all, please feel free to email me at con-tact@thedailysales.net.

Happy Social Selling!

RECOMMENDED READING

Listed below are a few Social Selling and Sales books that I highly recommend:

TOP SOCIAL SELLING BOOKS

COMBO Prospecting, Tony J Hughes

Social Selling Master, Jamie Shanks

Social Selling, Timothy Hughes

LinkedIn Unlocked, Melonie Dodaro

The LinkedIn Sales Playbook, Brynne Tillman

TOP SALES BOOKS

The Extremely Successful Salesman's Club, Chris Murray

The No.1 Best Seller, Lee Bartlett

Sales EQ, Jeb Blount (and every other Jeb Blount sales book—they're all incredible)

The Only Sales Guide You'll Ever Need, Anthony Iannarino

The Sales Bible, Jeffrey Gitomer

GAP Selling, Keenan

To Sell Is Human, Daniel Pink

The Perfect Close, James Muir

The Sales Development Playbook, Trish Bertuzzi

High Profit Prospecting, Mark Hunter

The 10X Rule, Grant Cardone

Selling From The Heart, Larry Levine

Everybody Works In Sales, Niraj Kapur

Secrets Of Successful Sales, Alison Edgar

Sales Success Stories, Scott Ingram

INDEX

1-Day LinkedIn Masterclass, 200

A

Account management, audio voice notes
    (usage), 128
Allen, Holly, 141
Always Be Connecting, 247
Always Be Consistent, 248
Always Be (Starting) Conversations, 248
Always Be Creating Content, 247
Approaches, variation, 53
Audio voice messages
    advice, 126–127
    brevity, importance, 126
    cold call follow-up, 138
    Cold Call, The, 138
    content, control, 127
    Content Reference, The, 135–136
    Event Invite, The, 137
    Expert Article, The, 138
    Free Offer, The, 137
    goals, 134
    number, control, 127
    opportunities, 127–128
    Planted Seed script, 134
    practice, importance, 126
    Profile Research, 134–135
    Real ROI Example, 136
    Referral, 135
    sending, 123–124

Thoughtful Gift, The, 139
tone, focus, 126
Audio voice notes
    basics, 141–146
    duration, maximum, 126
    effectiveness, 128
    emphasis, 130
    follow-up message, potential, 126
    inflection, consideration, 130
    pace, control, 130
    personalisation, 144
    relevance, importance, 129, 131
    sales scripts, 133
    script
        creation, 143
        straight reading, usage, 145
    sending
        process, 125
        timing, 128
    tone, importance, 129, 130–131
    usage, 24, 121
Audit, value, 137
Automation tools, 171–172
Auto-response, usage, 220
Away message, setting, 220

B

Background image, usage, 233
Best-Mitchell, Jarrod, 169
Billboard LinkedIn profile banner, creation, 227

INDEX

Blog
  sharing, 110
  writing, 90

C
Calendar Link, 44f
Call to action (CTA), 184
Capcut, usage, 173
Cards on the Table (message), usage, 97–98
Case Study Introduction (message)
  document, attachment (possibility), 92
  usage, 91–92
C-level prospects, ROI introduction (usage), 86
Clients
  achievement, proposal, 104
  post, recognition/compliment, 105–106
  potential ROI, display, 92–93
  reply, absence (reaction), 199
  thoughts/knowledge/experience, asking, 90
Closed deals, importance, 216
Close ratio, understanding, 214–215
Closing, audio voice notes (usage), 128
Cold calls/calling, 9, 110, 237
  admission/honesty, 101
  avoidance, 77
  Blockbuster, comparison, 238
  follow-up, audio voice message (usage), 138
  leveraging, 82–83
  LinkedIn InMails, comparison, 67–68
  problems, 10–11
  prospecting activity, 238
  receiving, 143
  sales strategy, weakness, 240
  social selling, contrast, 77, 204
  success rate, 199
  usage, 65
    fear, 205
  variation, 59
Cold Call, The (audio message script), 138
Cold emails, avoidance, 77
COMBO Prospecting (Hughes), 78
Communication
  method, 9
  platforms, plethora, 7–8
Company Follower, The (InMail sales
    template), 195
Congratulations message, usage, 155, 162
Connection
  Always Be Connection, 247
  message, personalisation, 56
  request, problems, 52
  validity, ensuring, 100
  video message, sending (reason), 170
Content
  creation, 16, 243–244, 247
  research, 29–30
  sharing, 16, 23, 164–165, 243–244
    engagement, opportunity, 110
    referencing, 99
  value, sharing, 113
Content Reference, The
  audio message script, 135–136
  video sales message script, 164–165
Conversation
  creation, 113
  navigation, 208
Conversation, initiation, 72
  content, sharing, 113
  opportunities, research, 30
  purpose, 79–80
  question, 46
Conversation-starting script, 136
Cover story video, addition, 218–219

D
Decision-makers
  attention, absence, 110
  busyness, 118
  cold call, usage, 66
  difficulty, 67
  emails, arrival/numbers, 93
  LinkedIn location, 67
  message, reading, 73
  phone communication, preference, 80
  printed material, impact, 95
  senior decision-makers, ROI introduction
    (usage), 86
Demo Offer (message), usage, 92–93
Did You Get My Letter? (message),
    usage, 102–103
Digital presence, 232
Digital sellers, digital customer needs, 80
Direct message, sending (connection,
    requirement), 68
Direct Profile View (message), usage, 109

E
eBook, offer/value, 95–96, 137
Effort, showing, 114
Ego boost, 164–165

Elevator pitch style profile summary, usage, 228

Emails, 239
    boxes, bombardment, 143
    follow-up email, usage, 136
    prospecting emails, sending, 122
    reply (absence), letter (sending), 202
    signature, profile link (addition), 230
    usage, 75, 110

Engagement
    social post engagement, 244
    social selling, 56–57

Engagement Thank You (message), usage, 109–111

Event Invitation (message)
    shortness, advantage, 94
    usage, 93–94

Event Invite, The (audio message script), 137

Events
    attendance, importance, 112
    search, 137

Expert Article, The
    InMail sales template, 185–186

Expert Article, The (audio message script), 138

Expert Insight, The (video sales message script), 165–166

Eye contact, importance, 166

F

Facebook, usage, 167

Face-to-face interaction, 89

Face-to-face meetings, 231
    variation, 59

First-degree connection, 51

First-degree direct connection, 183

Follow-up message, audio voice notes (usage), 126, 128, 138

Free Offer, The
    audio message script, 137
    InMail sales template, 191

Free Trial (message), usage, 92–93

Funding, receiving, 162

G

Gifting, power, 139

Going to the Same Event (message), usage, 111–112

H

Headline, creation, 234–235

"Here's MY Calendar Link" message, 43, 44f, 45

Honesty (message)
    Cards on the Table message, comparison, 101
    usage, 101–102

Honesty, power, 98, 103

Hughes, Tony J., 78

I

Inbound leads, 15
    generation, 14

Industry groups
    creation, 99
    joining, value, 99

Industry research document, offering (opportunity), 94

Industry whitepaper, company usage, 90

Information
    gathering, 90
    loading, avoidance, 74–75

InMails
    cold calls, comparison, 67–68
    content, aim, 184
    messages, 179
        contrast, 51–53
        responses, 173
    subject lines, 183
        usage, 221–222
    usage, payment/disadvantage, 180

InMail sales templates, 185
    Company Follower, The, 195
    Expert Article, The, 185–186
    Free Offer, The, 191
    InMail Video, The, 194
    New In-Role Message, The, 194
    Problem Solved, The, 193
    Referral, The, 187
    ROI Number, The, 189
    Straight to the Point, The, 188
    Testimonial, The, 190

InMail Video, The (InMail sales template), 194

Insights, value, 137

Instagram, usage, 167

Instant messaging, 239

Internal introduction, providing, 111

Introduction, The (video sales message script), 160

Introduction (message), usage, 84–85

L

Letters, sending, 202

Light message, usage, 88

LinkedIn
  activities, 242–243
  advice, 219
  audio voice messages. *See* Audio voice messages.
  audio voice notes. *See* Audio voice notes.
  content, creation/sharing, 16
  groups, problems, 99
  InMail. *See* InMails.
  invitation (acceptance), personal note (inclusion), 69
  leveraging, 203, 242
  network, daily growth, 97
  Sales Navigator. *See* Sales Navigator.
  time expenditure, 252
  video messages. *See* Video messages; Video sales message script.
LinkedIn messages
  advice, 117
  aggressiveness, avoidance, 73, 77
  brevity, avoidance, 41–42, 42f
  case study document, attachment (possibility), 92
  excess, problem, 31–35
  goal, 82–84
  information, loading (avoidance), 74–75
  InMail, contrast, 51–53
  length, avoidance, 39, 40f
  leveraging, 204
  overcomplication, problems, 73
  personalisation, 22, 56, 82
  power, 18
  response
    absence, 21
    rate, increase, 23
  sending
    fear/absence, 3–4
    timing, 55
  seven-figure LinkedIn message, 65
  softer language, success, 83
  templates
    learning, 80
    types, 81
LinkedIn profile
  accomplishments/interests, listing, 236
  articles/activity, presence, 234
  background image, usage, 233
  building, 231
  cover story video, addition, 220–221
  creation, 232
  headline, creation, 234–235
  link, addition, 223, 228
  "My Network" section, examination, 96
  photo, usage, 229
  recommendations, 235
  skills/endorsements, 235
  summary section, usage, 234
  URL, customisation, 229–230
  viewing, 107
  views, examination (regularity), 107–108, 225
  visiting, 105
  work experience, listing, 235–236
LinkedIn Profile Video, The (video sales message script), 163–164
  personalisation, 164
LinkedIn Recommended You (message), usage, 96–97
Links, recordkeeping, 222
Looking for Leadership Insight (message), usage, 90–91

M
Media, attachment, 234
Missed Call (message), usage, 115–116
Motivation, growth, 4
Mutual Connection/Referral (message), usage, 100–101

N
Network
  growth, 243
  research/qualification, 114–115
Networking, key event attendance (importance), 112
New In-Role Message, The (InMail sales template), 192
Newsletter, initiation, 224
Notification bell, location, 154

O
Offer, value/knowledge/insight, 94
Official referral, 135
Opportunity
  celebration, 218
  conversation, 207
  qualification, 217
Outbound leads, generation, 14
Outbound social selling, 13

P

Pattern interruption, 34
Personal brands, 232
Personalisation, importance/equation, 25, 164
Phone calls, 9
    arrangement, 17–18, 111
    decision-maker preferences, 80
    follow-up/receiving, 76
    occurrence, 108
    usage, 201–202, 203
Photo, sharing, 224, 233, 243–244
Pipedrive CRM, usage, 222
Pipelines
    absence, impact, 217
    building, 217
    denial, 215
    feeding, continuation, 217
    honesty, impact, 215
    importance, 213, 216–217
    shrinkage, 216
Pitch message, conversion, 136
Pitch slapping, 55
Planted Seed (audio message script), 134
Posts
    commenting, 228
    engagement, 23
    recognition/compliment, 105–106
    sharing, 200
    social post engagement, 244
    testimonial post, sharing, 221
    writing, 228–229
Problem Solved, The (InMail sales
        template), 193
Problem Solver (message), usage, 87–88
Profile Research (audio message script),
        134–135
Profile View (message)
    sending/reply, 108
    usage, 106–108
Proposal, presentation, 76–77
Prospecting
    activity, 242
    audio voice notes, effectiveness, 128
    channels/platforms/tools, 9
    gifting, power, 139
    key event attendance, importance, 112
    maze, 8–10, 8f
    messages, advice, 133–134
    opportunity, 102, 216–218

Prospecting emails, sending, 122
Prospects
    conversation, initiation, 72–73
    conversion, 102–103
    differences, 10
    directness, requirement, 71
    level (increase), personalisation increase
        (requirement), 69–70
    LinkedIn profiles, visiting, 105
    message
        backfiring, 100–101
        sending, 163
    messaging, scenarios, 208–209
    methods, 7–8
    number, maximum (reaching), 12
    personalization, 70–71
    posts, links (recordkeeping), 222
    potential, qualification, 108
    pre-qualification, 117–118
    reassurance, 187
    reply, absence (reaction), 199
    research, business value, 26
    searching, 247
    treatment, 60
    video message, sending, 222–223
    voice notes, usage, 143

Q

QR code, usage, 141, 146
Question, form (usage), 88

R

Rapport, building, 17, 209
Reachdesk, usage, 139
Real ROI Example (audio message script), 136
Recent Activity Observation (message),
        usage, 105–106
Referral process, 236
Referral, The
    audio message script, 135
    InMail sales template, 185
    video sales message script, 165
Relationships, building, 167
Relevance, importance/equation, 25
Replies, absence (reasons), 21
Research
    advanced research, 28–29
    content, defining, 29–30
    depth, 28

Research (*continued*)
importance/equation, 25
locations, 27–29
relevance, ensuring, 162
Research Reference, The (video sales message script), 161–162
Research (message), usage, 114–115
Revenue, generation, 106
ROI Introduction (message), usage, 85–87
ROI Number, The (InMail sales template), 189
ROI Question (message), usage, 104–105

S
Sales
absence, pipeline absence (impact), 217
celebration, 218
closing, 246
conversations, initiation, 208
desire, 11
discussion, 17
emails, variation, 59
focus, 245
honesty/upfrontness, power, 98
love, 4
managers, honesty, 218
opportunity
celebration, 215–216
closing, 202
creation, 18
generation, 215–216
pipelines, 213–214
reality, 11–12
representative, connection, 17
success, pipeline honesty (impact), 215
teams, leading, 213
value, 208
research duration, comparison, 27
video messages, usage, 153
Sales development representatives (SDRs)
hiring, 193
training, 141
Sales email, crafting, 75–76
Sales Navigator
advice, 219–224
usage, 174, 179–180
Salespeople, training, 4–5
Sales pitch
avoidance, 71
sending, question, 46

Second-degree connection, Connect option, 68
Sendoso, usage, 139
Senior decision-makers, ROI introduction (usage), 86
Seven-figure LinkedIn message, 65
scene, setting, 65
Shared LinkedIn Group (message), usage, 98–99
Sharing Content (message), usage, 113
Similar Company Insight, The (video sales message script), 164
small to medium-sized employers (SMEs), selling, 65–66
Social marketing, 15
Social media
enjoyment, 248
profiles, 232
usage, 10, 242–243
effectiveness, 246
Social post engagement, 244
Social profiles, attitude, 231
Social selling, 241
advice, 227–230
basics, 245
dance, 56–57
inbound-generating activity, comparison, 13
opportunity creation, 77–78
outbound-lead-generating platform, potential, 13–14
phone/cold calling, contrast, 77, 204
process, 78–79
push, 14
stigma, 203
success, 248
usage, 18
Social Selling Podcast, The (Best-Mitchell), 169
Soft call to action (soft CTA), 144
Softer language, success, 83
Soft introduction-style message, 87
Spam folder, email delivery, 93
Spam messages, dislike, 37–38
Spamming, 55
Spammy messages, defining/avoidance, 38, 72, 115, 183
Spammy pitches, avoidance, 45
Sponsor, promotion, 136
Spray and pray, 55
Straight-to-pitch approach, 47
Straight to the Point (InMail sales template), 190
Subject lines, usage, 221–222

Subtitles/captions, usage, 89
Summary section, usage, 230

T
Targets, reaching (opportunities), 214–215
Template, usage (problem), 26
Testimonial post, sharing, 221
Testimonial, The (InMail sales template), 190
Text-based messages, sending
        (limitations), 23–24
Third-degree connection, Message button
        (usage), 68
Thoughtful Gift, The
    audio message script, 139
    deep research, requirement, 167
    video sales message script, 167
TikTok, usage, 167
Tone of voice, friendliness, 144
Toys "R" Us, failure, 239
Training video, value, 137
Transactional purchase, 207
Twitter, usage, 167

U
Upfrontness, power, 98, 103
URL, customisation, 229–230

V
Video DMs, usage (opportunity), 174
Video messages, 149
    advantage, 89
    advice, 174
    automation tools, 171–172
    background, simplicity, 173
    brevity, importance, 172
    camera
        addressing, 172
        lens, cleaning, 174
    content, uncertainty, 171
    effectiveness, 149
    eye contact, importance, 166
    name, stating, 172
    performance, 156
    personalisation, 170
    pitching, control, 172
    reciprocity, 171
    replies, 155
    sales, conclusion, 153
    script, 175–176

sending, 169, 170–176, 223
sharing, 154
subtitles/captions, usage, 89
usage, 24, 88–89
    fear, overcoming, 150–151
value, 150
vanity, impact, 171
Video sales messages scripts, 159
    Expert Insight, The, 165–166
    Introduction, The, 160
    LinkedIn Profile Video, The, 163–164
    positive tone, usage, 160
    Referral, The, 165
    Research Reference, The, 161–162
    research, relevance (ensuring), 162
    Similar Company Insight, The, 166
    Thoughtful Gift, The, 167
    Website Browse, The, 162–163
    Whiteboard, The, 160–161
Videos, sharing, 229
Video, usage, 239
Vidyard, usage, 162–163, 175
Voicemails, usage, 110
Voice notes
    personalisation, 144
    prospect dislike, 145
    script, creation, 143
    sending, simplicity, 142
    usage, 24, 121, 142–146

W
Webinar, usage/value, 136, 137
Website Browse, The (video sales message
        script), 162–163
Whiteboard, The (video sales message
        script), 160–161
    creativity, 161
Whiteboard, usage, 173, 174
Words, usage (softness), 83
Work experience, listing, 235–236
Would You Like an Ebook (message), usage, 95–96
Written messages
    advice, 117
    reply, 156–157

Y
You're Using Our Competitor (message)
    upfrontness/honesty, 103
    usage, 103–104